Deep Sea Chanties

Also from Westphalia Press
westphaliapress.org

The Idea of the Digital University
France and New England Volumes 1, 2, & 3
Treasures of London
The History of Photography
L'Enfant and the Freemasons
Baronial Bedrooms
Making Trouble for Muslims
Material History and Ritual Objects
Paddle Your Own Canoe
Opportunity and Horatio Alger
Careers in the Face of Challenge
Bookplates of the Kings
Collecting American Presidential Autographs
Freemasonry in Old Buffalo
Young Freemasons?
Social Satire and the Modern Novel
The Essence of Harvard
Ivanhoe Masonic Quartettes
A Definitive Commentary on Bookplates
James Martineau and Rebuilding Theology
No Bird Lacks Feathers
Gilded Play
Earthworms, Horses, and Living Things
The Man Who Killed President Garfield

Anti-Masonry and the Murder of Morgan
Understanding Art
Homeopathy
Fishing the Florida Keys
Collecting Old Books
Masonic Secret Signs and Passwords
The Thomas Starr King Dispute
Earl Warren's Masonic Lodge
Lariats and Lassos
Mr. Garfield of Ohio
The Wisdom of Thomas Starr King
The French Foreign Legion
War in Syria
Naturism Comes to the United States
New Sources on Women and Freemasonry
Designing, Adapting, Strategizing in Online Education
Gunboat and Gun-runner
Zigzagging
Natural Gas as an Instrument of Russian State Power
World Food Policy
New Frontiers in Criminology
Feeding the Global South
Benjamin Franklin and Canada

Deep Sea Chanties Old Sea Songs

Edited by Frank Shay
Decorations and Woodcuts by
Edw. A. Wilson
Introduction by William McFee

WESTPHALIA PRESS
An imprint of Policy Studies Organization

Deep Sea Chanties: Old Sea Songs
All Rights Reserved © 2017 by Policy Studies Organization

Westphalia Press
An imprint of Policy Studies Organization
1527 New Hampshire Ave., NW
Washington, D.C. 20036
info@ipsonet.org

ISBN-13: 978-1-63391-510-7
ISBN-10: 1-63391-510-7

Cover design by Jeffrey Barnes:
jbarnesbook.design

Daniel Gutierrez-Sandoval, Executive Director
PSO and Westphalia Press

Updated material and comments on this edition
can be found at the Westphalia Press website:
www.westphaliapress.org

This new edition is dedicated to
India D'Avignon,
lifelong champion of the importance of
music in our daily lives

Printed in the United States of America

DEEP SEA CHANTIES

Old Sea Songs

EDITED BY FRANK SHAY

DECORATIONS AND WOODCUTS BY
EDW. A. WILSON

INTRODUCTION BY WILLIAM McFEE

LONDON
WM. HEINEMANN, LTD.
1925

ACKNOWLEDGMENT

THE first wood blocks that were cut for "Deep Sea Chanties" have gravitated toward the end of the book, so in the Chinese fashion this, my last job, will appear at the beginning.

First I want to thank Mr. Robert J. Clark, of Boston, who allowed me the use of his collection of House Flags; Mr. Basil Lubbock for writing his three fine books, "Blackwall Frigates," "China Clippers," and "Colonial Clippers," and Commander Robinson for "The British Tar in Fact and Fiction." Other sources of information were the *Mariner's Mirror*, Cruikshank's drawings for Dibdin's "Sea Songs," *Illustrated London News* of the early '50's, Masefield's "Sea Life in Nelson's Time" and "The Sailors' Garland."

EDW. A. WILSON.

Truro, Mass.
May 6, 1924.

CONTENTS

	PAGE
Introduction	xi
Foreword	xix
AWAY, RIO!	1
A-CRUISING WE WILL GO	8
SPANISH LADIES	10
JACK THE GUINEA PIG	21
THE DEAD HORSE	24
COME ROLL HIM OVER	29
CAPTAIN BOVER	30
HAND OVER HAND	35
DOO ME AMA	36
EARLY IN THE MORNING	39
BLOW THE MAN DOWN	45
ACROSS THE WESTERN OCEAN	46
LOWLANDS	48
THE BLACK-BALL LINE	49
ROLL THE COTTON DOWN	55
THE WIDE MISSOURI	56
THE MAID OF AMSTERDAM	57
THE *GEORGE ALOE*	58
BLOW, BULLIES, BLOW	71
CAPTAIN KIDD	73
CHEER'LY O!	75
HANGING JOHNNY	81
WHISKY FOR MY JOHNNY	82

CONTENTS

	PAGE
TOMMY'S GONE TO HILO	83
BONEY	84
SALLY BROWN	85
THE PLAINS OF MEXICO	91
HAUL AWAY, JOE	92
JOHNNY BOKER	97
HIGH BARBAREE	98
REUBEN RANZO	100
WE'RE ALL BOUND TO GO	102
STORM-ALONG	108
PADDY DOYLE	114
A LONG TIME AGO	115
CHEER'LY MAN	117
ROLL AND GO	119
POOR OLD JOE	120
"I AM A BRISK AND SPRIGHTLY LAD"	121
BEN BACKSTAY	123
THE BANKS OF THE SACRAMENTO	126
HAUL THE BOWLINE	132
GOOD-BYE, FARE YOU WELL	133
HOMEWARD BOUND	135
ONE DAY MORE	141
ROLLING HOME TO MERRIE ENGLAND	143
IT'S TIME FOR US TO LEAVE HER, JOHNNY	145
Notes	147

KEEP ON

FOREWORD

IN bringing these songs together I have sought to catch for the moment the spirit of the men of the clipper-ship era. That glorious period, marked roughly by the Mexican War and the California gold rush, is finding perpetuation in the enthusiasms of those who love the sea and ships. Ship models, romances and tales of the sea, log books and nautical instruments so eagerly sought after by these enthusiasts are, after all, but outward symbols of the men who trod the decks and warped and reefed the sails. Those deeds were not accomplished without song and the songs they sang were from their own souls: not written for them by poets and ballad-mongers. In reading them we are made privy not only to the singer but to the audience: their thoughts, their lives, and their environment.

Poets have written and will continue to write of the sea, of shipwrecks and rescues, but it is only from the chanty and the forebitter that we really enter into the lives of these men. Not of brave deeds nor of glorious battles do they make song, these were left to the man-o'-war's-man. The a. b.'s of those days were concerned mostly with ports of call, sweethearts, liquor, and home. Of these they sang lustily.

Roughly the songs may be divided into two classes: songs of work and songs of leisure. To the former belongs the chanty. The ballad, or forebitter, is the song for between watches.

There are many kinds of chanties, a chanty for every duty, and the order to *heave and chanty* brought redoubled efforts and made them lighter. Literally there are but three kinds of chanties: capstan chantys, used in warping or weighing anchor or hoisting sails; the halyard, or long-drag chanty, used at topsails and top-gallant sails; the sheet, tack, and bowline chanties, more often known as short-drag chantys, were used when the fore, main, or cross-jack sheets were hauled aft and bowlines tautened and made fast. Other chanties, such as hand-over-hand and pumping chanties, explain themselves.

The ballads were, as a rule, called *forebitters*, taking their name from the stage or platform on which the singer or soloist took his place, the forebitts, a hardy construction of wood near the foremast through which many of the main ropes were fed. In this manner he was raised some three or four feet above his fellows, who squatted about on kegs and coils of rope. He had no accompaniment, though often the watch joined in on the chorus.

Neither chanties nor forebitters were ever written down. They varied greatly according to the soloist and chantyman. They began with regulation verses and carried on as long as the task lasted. If further verses were required the chantyman improvised, taking, very often, some incident that had occurred on shore and with which the crew was familiar. He had only to trust to his imagination: the versification was simple and there was much latitude as to rhymes and metre, and most of the airs would sound monotonous to ears accustomed to more highly developed music.

If I have succeeded in catching the spirit of a glorious and departed period of merchant shipping it is due in no small way to the enthusiasm of Mr. Christopher Morley and to the patient help of Mr. Eugene O'Neill and Mr. Harry Kemp. It is a pleasure to acknowledge their help and interest.

FRANK SHAY.

PROVINCETOWN, MASS.
February 14, 1924.

INTRODUCTION

WHILE the collection of deep-sea songs herein presented stands easily enough without superfluous eulogium, there is something to be said for an attempt to explain these chanties as authentic vestiges of a way of life and an outlook upon the visible and spiritual world that have of necessity receded from the ocean with the advance of mechanical means of propulsion. For it must be remembered that while a sailing ship may be regarded by a theorist as a mechanism, the actual fact is that ships under sail and steered by men are not machines at all but sentient beings of which the master, the seamen, the masts, and sails and cordage are organs of a living whole. In more than a merely fanciful sense the winds of heaven blow into her the breath of life. Her very sounds and complainings are widely divergent from the sounds of machinery; the moods she inspires, the affections and hatreds, lie in the regions of human society and polity;

INTRODUCTION

and the edifice of fond and fantastic legends that has been built up around the central phenomenon of the sailing ship and her crew stands alone in the world to-day as a remarkable survival of those accretions once common to every guild and craft, from soldier to magician.

It is necessary to emphasize the passing of the seaman's songs because, while many of us alive to-day have heard them, and participated in joyous evenings devoted to an apparently interminable series of roaring choruses, we are not likely to hear them from the throats of the young men of the modern mercantile marine, and still less from the modern bluejacket. There are many reasons for this apart from steam and wireless. A seaman is only a landsman trained to float, and the modern world is based upon conceptions of honour, economic responsibility, and commercial organization very different from the world in which the sailor shipped in an old-time vessel for a voyage to the West Coast, to China, or the Antipodes. Of necessity an enormous portion of a seaman's life was spent on ships and in foreign parts. He became one of a distinctive type. His voice, his gait, his diction, his tattooing, his clothes, and his unfortunate conviviality—which last was one of the famous "rewards of abstinence" discovered by the political economists—all placed him immediately among men, and in no way was his collective personality expressed so powerfully as in his songs, with their curious persistence through a series of generations; their metre, which was sometimes comprehended with difficulty by the untrained ear; and their subjects, which were a wild blend of superstition, rough humour, and tender sentiments.

All this, it is pointed out, is now no more than a memory. The seaman of to-day has a gramophone which grinds out the current syncopations and sentimentalisms. A hydro-electric mechanism draws up his heavy anchors with the power and precision of a giant crane. His vessel has neither rigging nor sails, but proceeds upon a course as inexorable as a main road. Indeed, the routes of steamships

INTRODUCTION

have adopted the phrase, "ocean highway," and a prize fight in Havana may be reported and discussed on board of a vessel in the China Seas a few hours after the knock-out. And so there is a very real and valuable reason for collecting those sea songs which are the sailor's expression of himself; his contribution to art, which is only "artless" because it is unconscious and the pure revelation of untutored souls. A true chanty is as authentic as a saga, and like a saga it is composed independent of the written word; it is handed on from one votary to another like a prophecy, a legend, or a tradition. It arises out of the sailor's relations to the elements, to the land, and to his companions. It is often a grotesque anticipation of the truth recently discovered by solemn scientific welfare workers—that men work better while singing. Like the mediæval church, it comprises within itself the spiritual and emotional life of humble folk. A good chantyman was regarded in the same way as the bards and glee-men of an earlier day ashore. Like the old ballads and early religious art, perspective and logic are not essential to truth and beauty, and the emotions communicated by the singing of seamen untrammelled by self-consciousness are not to be evoked by literary compositions, which bear the same relation to the natural chanty that Tennyson's "smooth imitations," as Emerson called them, bear to "Morte d'Arthur."

It is because of this discrepancy between the oral original and the undeniably brilliant renderings of modern poets that the present writer emphasizes the vanishing opportunity to hear the former. It would be a mistake to imagine that chanties died out immediately with the incursions of the steamer. The old-style tramp, with her tendency toward inefficiency and her adventurous combats with her heavy weather and unprofitable freights, inspired her company with some of the affection and bitterness so often expressed by sailors for their square-rigged homes. Moreover, her officers were nearly always ex-sailing-ship men. Time had gilded their austere ap-

INTRODUCTION

prenticeships with a marvellous glamour, and on fine evenings in the Indian Ocean the second mate's cabin became the chamber of a remarkable harmony. It was under such circumstances that the present writer learned some of the chanties included in this present collection, with many notable verses of necessity omitted in a volume purporting to be read by the general public. Here again we encounter a singular identity of the chanty with the fundamental folklore of the illiterate human. There is a naïve innocence of heart about even the unavailable chanties that is in striking contrast to the sophisticated nastiness of modern innuendoes. One is reminded of Sterne's rejoinder to the lady, and also of that body of humour known as Elizabethan. A sailor's method of telling a story is as direct as a bullet, and it is not surprising that his songs should have the same quality. But the Rabelaisian factor was never a predominating one. The seaman, for all his robust ideas of enjoyment and his inevitable slips into mire, was easily deflected into a species of hilarious virtue, and like the peasants of the soil, he had no genius for sensuous introspection. And he had too much to pour into his uncouth songs to find room for the unsavoury lucubrations of conscious unregenerates.

And reflecting upon the essential poetry and beauty of chanties, the present writer is reminded of an incident which probably afforded him his last experience of the kind. He recalls a certain commander of a naval vessel during the war, whom we may call Captain Jones, since that is very nearly his name. There was a large crew aboard that ship, a crew including many ratings of a type that must have oppressed their captain by their incongruous grouping under his eye. They were wireless signalmen, aircraft mechanics, and manipulators of strange guns. These and their officers, clean-cut youths of modern type and gentle birth, regarded the old gentleman with a mingled affection and pride. For he, after a long career in sailing

INTRODUCTION

ships and steamers, had come back into the game from a comfortable retirement, and he could in no wise accustom himself to the intricate ceremonial of naval discipline. "Divisions" were a burden to his soul, and the daily court for defaulters took him into a maze of casuistry. He would turn with relief to his cabin, and he could be heard in the bathroom, while he delighted his stout old heart with washing his socks, humming "Blow, boys, blow" with an occasional rendition, in a husky basso, of "Nearer, my God, to Thee," for he was devout as well, and we were aware of his passion for prayer meetings.

The particular time of this particular episode was a Christmas party in a Mediterranean port, a time when the officers of a naval vessel are permitted to unbend and mingle with the ratings on the lower deck. There were many talents on that ship, and when we descended to the 'tween-deck flat, it was to assist at a notable concert. There was a certain amount of irrelevant conviviality going on. Some heroes were already fallen into remarkable poses and others were inconveniently vocal. The main function, however, was a success. With the Commander sitting placidly in our midst we listened to and applauded the stars who occupied the impromptu stage. There was the "O. D.," a sailor of about eighteen, with an extraordinarily alert and suspicious countenance, who sang "Sing Me to Sleep" without inspiring any confidence in his audience. There was the surgeon-commander, copiously wined, who recited "The Ballad of the Clamperdown" in a hissing monotone that caused an unseen but intoxicated stoker to moan profanely and so evoke irresistible hilarity. There was the Lower Deck Comic, an aircraft C.P.O., whose flexile and lugubrious features became a miracle of unloveliness as he imitated George Robey. And there was the ward-room waiter, an enormous and shambling figure in a dress suit of maroon plush, with an aged kit-bag into which we were invited to pack up our troubles and embark upon an eternal smile.

INTRODUCTION

Doubtless it was a merely formal and diplomatic courtesy that inspired the master of ceremonies to call upon our Commander to amuse the company, for he had revealed no gift of that kind in the past. We had almost forgotten him, sitting so quietly in an armchair in front, his round stout figure filling it to capacity, his hands folded in his lap, his shining bald head and short white beard concealed by the rest of the officers about him. And it was with some self-consciousness and trepidation that we applauded as he rose and stepped upon the stage. We wondered, most of us, what he would do.

Captain Jones stood there for a moment, his mild blue eyes, like those of a child, regarding the smiling audience not at all. They seemed indeed to be fixed upon infinity or the distant past, the days ere we were born. He took no notice at all of the accompanist, who awaited with tense interest some hint of the song to come. But the Commander was in no need of an accompanist. Indeed, there was none there to keep him company; for he suddenly began to roar out a deep-sea chanty. The volume of sound in that lower-deck place was formidable. It filled the far spaces where men lay prone, and brought them to their feet in wonder. It shook the hearts of young men who had been born into an age of mechanism and so knew nothing of "hempen bridle and horse of tree," of the long voyages and the sea's relentless enmity. There was in it a touch of terror and strangeness, as though we heard the voice of a man from another century singing a song born of sorrow and toil, with a vision of the earth as a great ocean of tribulation, with fair havens of deceptive felicity and bewildering complexity. It was as though an Elizabethan spirit had taken possession of our "old man" and he was revealing to us the secrets of an obscure and tormented soul. And suddenly, as we sat tense and unhappy, he ceased and stood looking steadily into infinite distance.

And to an observant witness the problem was not so much what that startling old man was thinking of as he stood there, as what the

INTRODUCTION

young men might be seeing when they regarded him. Even when, without warning, Captain Jones began to sing, as though to himself, a very different kind of song—"The Voice of Her I Love"—he was revealing to us a psychology and a sentiment destined to vanish in a decade. To us he was coeval with "The Beggars' Opera" and the novels of Marryat and Cooper. And when he stepped, almost in absence of mind, from the dais to his seat among us, we were aware of the inadequacy of our applause. Perhaps we had a shadowy feeling that we should not look upon his like again.

It would be an error, however, for the general landsman-reader to imagine that all seamen were singers of chanties. Indeed, the reverse was the case. The sailor was, in spite of his reputation as a roisterer, a quiet and retiring character ashore and at sea, until roused by liquor and good company. He was, in fact, a peasant afloat, and his characteristics were fundamentally those of a peasant; just as the stokers of ships, who draw their crews from the country districts of Spain and Italy, resemble peasants in hell when they toil in front of their enormous fires. There is in the sailor's song, as in his yarns, a non-literary exuberance, using the word literary in its more precious and sophisticated sense. An example of the latter mode imported into a sea song may be found in the correct verses frequently grafted upon a vigorous original, as in "Rolling Home":

> *Up aloft amid the rigging*
> *Sings the loud exultant gale—*

which may be verse, but is no true chanty language. Seamen were quick to detect these gratuitous emendments to their songs and would have none of them. Indeed, the spirit of the chanty is beyond the reach of all who have not been seamen. There is a divine homeliness in the chantyman's imagery, an extravagant simplicity, that can only be compared with the art of the Primitives and the Percy

INTRODUCTION

Reliques of Ballad Poetry. He is an improvisator with an elvish twist in his humour that makes him free of the company of saints and sinners. He delights in impossible, or rather improbable, exaggerations, and he moves easily from the humble sphere of the forecastle to the vasty regions of apocalyptic happenings. It is a view of a familiar yet marvellous world that we obtain through the eyes and hearts of the old-time seaman. For him the great fabric of our civilizations, our high politics and fermenting philosophies, were but the distant and unexplored ranges beyond the seacoast of Bohemia. Out of the austere materials at his command he has fashioned his idylls and his pastorals, his sagas and ballads. And those who approach the recorded fragments of his poesie with sympathy and understanding will become aware, beneath the labouring heave and beat of the metre, beneath the uncouth mumblings and cries, of a sweetness and depth of humanity unsurpassed in our time, a clear light of the soul shining upon the dark and turbulent waters of the world.

WILLIAM McFEE.

AWAY, RIO!

O, the anchor is weighed, and the sails they are set,
Away, Rio!
The maids that we're leaving we'll never forget,
For we're bound for the Rio Grande,
And away, Rio! aye, Rio!
Sing fare-ye-well, my bonny young gel,
For we're bound for the Rio Grande!

So man the good capstan, and run it around,
Away, Rio!
We'll heave up the anchor to this jolly sound,
For we're bound for the Rio Grande,
And away, Rio! aye, Rio!
Sing fare-ye-well, my bonny young gel,
For we're bound for the Rio Grande!

We've a jolly good ship, and a jolly good crew,
Away, Rio!
A jolly good mate, and a good skipper, too,
For we're bound for the Rio Grande,
And away, Rio! aye, Rio!
Sing fare-ye-well, my bonny young gel,
For we're bound for the Rio Grande!

We'll sing as we heave to the maidens we leave,
Away, Rio!
And you who are listening, good-bye to you,
For we're bound for Rio Grande,
And away, Rio! aye, Rio!
Sing fare-ye-well, my bonny young gel,
For we're bound for the Rio Grande!
Come heave up the anchor, let's get it aweigh,
Away, Rio!
It's got a firm grip, so heave steady, I say,
For we're bound for the Rio Grande,
And away, Rio! aye, Rio!
Sing fare-ye-well, my bonny young gel,
We're bound for the Rio Grande!

REELING 'M OFF

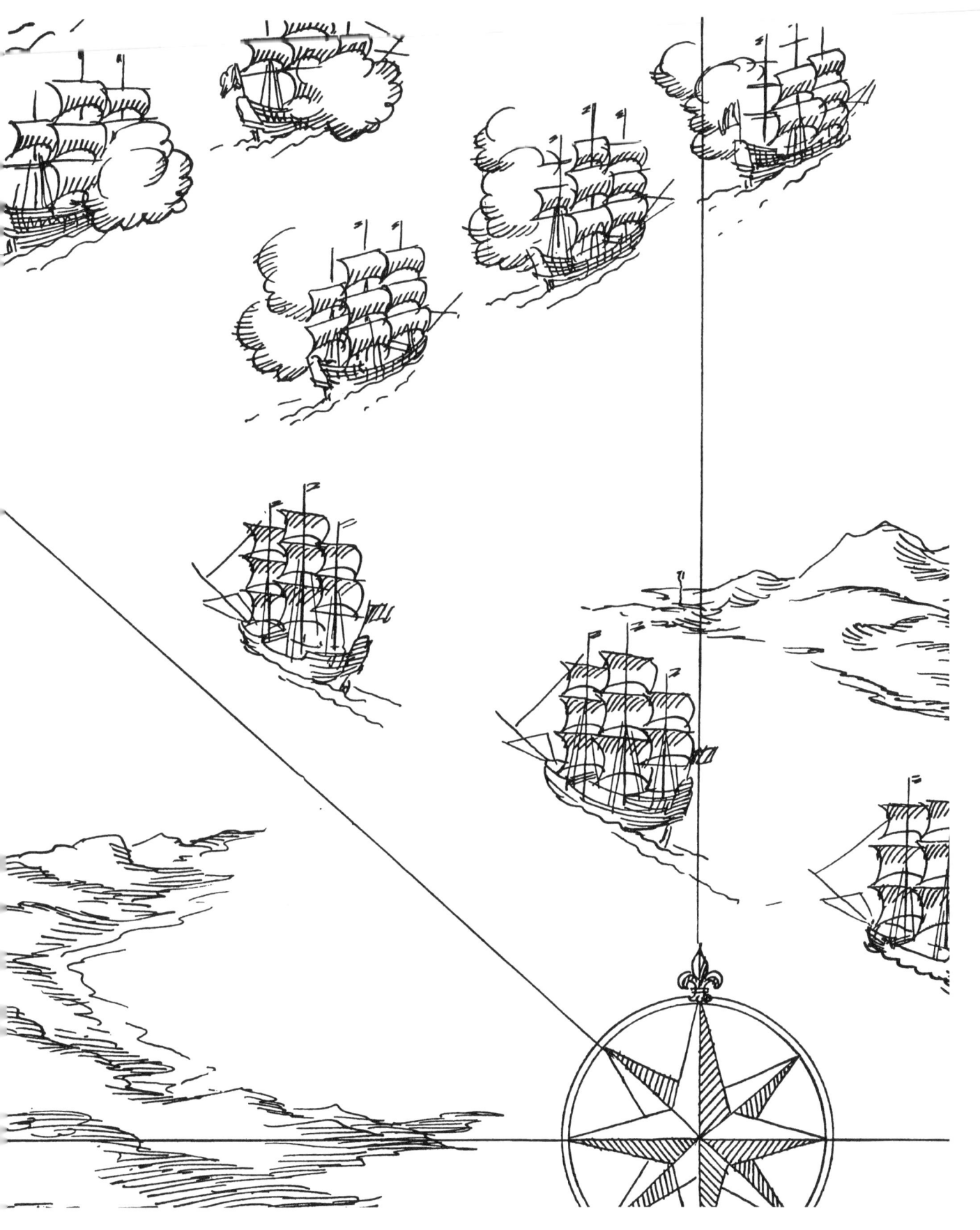

Heave with a will, and heave long and strong,
Away, Rio!
Sing a good chorus, for 'tis a good song,
For we're bound for the Rio Grande,
And away, Rio! aye, Rio!
Sing fare-ye-well, my bonny young gel,
For we're bound for the Rio Grande!

Heave only one pawl, then 'vast heaving, belay!
Away, Rio!
Heave steady, because we say farewell to-day,
For we're bound for the Rio Grande,
And away, Rio! aye, Rio!
Sing fare-ye-well, my bonny young gel,
For we're bound for the Rio Grande!

The chain's up and down, now the bosun did say,
Away, Rio!
Heave up to the hawse-pipe, the anchor's aweigh,
For we're bound for the Rio Grande,
And away, Rio! aye, Rio!
Sing fare-ye-well, my bonny young gel,
We're bound for the Rio Grande!

A-CRUISING WE WILL GO

Behold upon the swelling seas
With streaming pennants gay,
Our gallant ship invites the waves,
While glory leads the way.

And a-cruising we will go—oho, oho, oho,
And a-cruising we will go—oho, oho, oho,
And a-cruising we will go—o—oho,
And a-cruising we will go.

Ye beauteous maids, your smiles bestow,
For if you prove unkind,
How can we hope to beat the foe?
We leave our hearts behind.

When a-cruising we will go—oho, oho, oho,
When a-cruising we will go—oho, oho, oho,
When a-cruising we will go—o—oho,
When a-cruising we will go.

See Hardy's flag once more display'd,
Upon the deck he stands;
Britannia's glory ne'er can fade,
Or tarnish in his hands.

So a-cruising we will go—oho, oho, oho,
So a-cruising we will go—oho, oho, oho,
So a-cruising we will go—o—oho,
So a-cruising we will go.

Britain to herself but true,
To France defiance hurl'd:
Give peace, America, with you,
And war with all the world.

And a-cruising we will go—oho, oho, oho,
And a-cruising we will go—oho, oho, oho,
And a-cruising we will go—o—oho,
And a-cruising we will go.

SPANISH LADIES

Farewell and adieu to you, gay Spanish ladies,
Farewell and adieu to you, ladies of Spain,
For we've received orders for to sail to old England;
But we hope very soon we shall see you again.

We'll rant and we'll roar like true British sailors,
We'll rant and we'll roar across the salt seas,
Until we strike soundings in the channel of old England,
From Ushant to Scilly is thirty-five leagues.

Then we hove our ship to with the wind at sou'-west, my boys,
We hove our ship to our soundings for to see;
So we rounded and sounded, and got forty-five fathoms,
We squared our mainyard, up channel steered we.

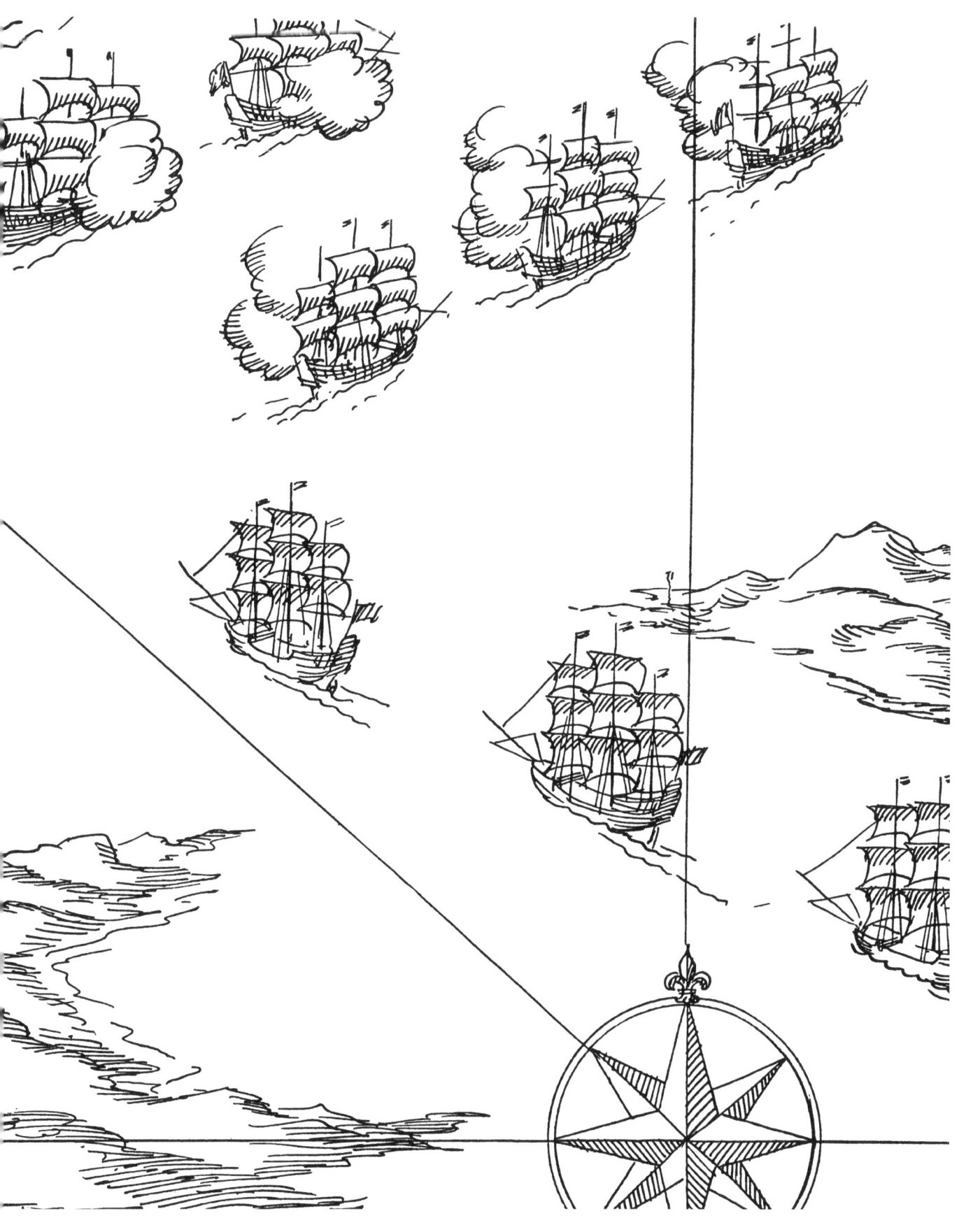

We'll rant and we'll roar like true British sailors,
We'll rant and we'll roar across the salt seas,
Until we strike soundings in the channel of old England,
From Ushant to Scilly is thirty-five leagues.

Now the first land we made it is called the Deadman,
Then Ram Head off Plymouth, Start, Portland, and Wight;
We sailed by Beachy, by Fairlee and Dungeness,
Until we came abreast of the South Foreland Light.

We'll rant and we'll roar like true British sailors,
We'll rant and we'll roar across the salt seas,
Until we strike soundings in the channel of old England,
From Ushant to Scilly is thirty-five leagues.

Then the signal was made for the grand fleet for to anchor,
All in the Downs that night for to meet;
Then it's stand by your stoppers, let go your shank painters,
Haul all your clew garnets, stick out tacks and sheets.

We'll rant and we'll roar like true British sailors,
We'll rant and we'll roar across the salt seas,
Until we strike soundings in the channel of old England,
From Ushant to Scilly is thirty-five leagues.

Now let every man toss off a full bumper,
And let every man toss off a full bowl;
And we'll drink and be merry and drown melancholy,
Singing, here's a good health to all true-hearted souls.

THE GIRL HE LEFT BEHIND

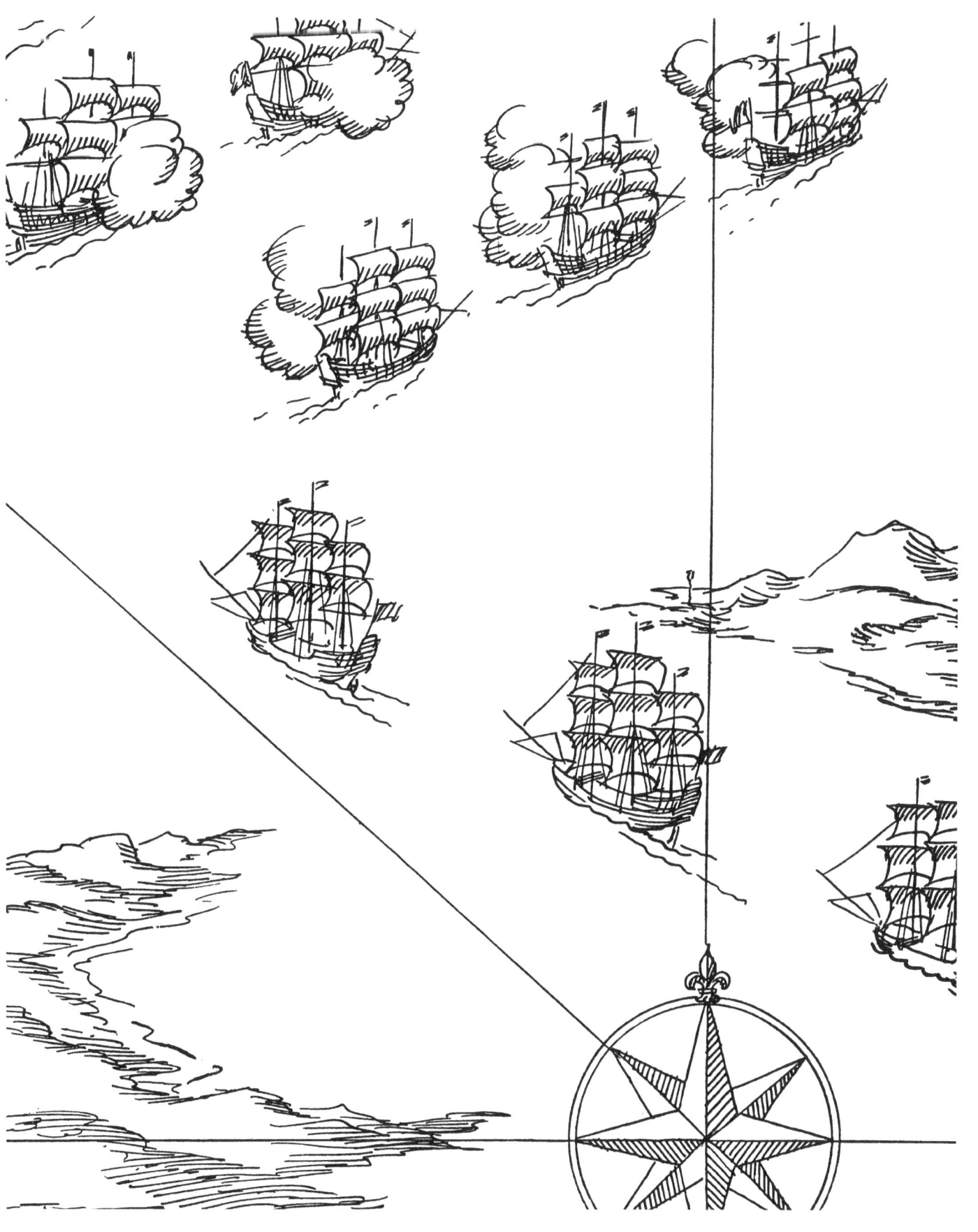

JACK THE GUINEA PIG

When the anchor's weigh'd and the ship's unmoored,
And the landsmen lag behind, sir,
The sailor joyful skips on board,
And, swearing, prays for a wind, sir:
Towing here,
Yehoing there,
Steadily, readily,
Cheerily, merrily,
Still from care and thinking free,
Is a sailor's life, at sea.

When we sail with a fresh'ning breeze,
And the landsmen all grow sick, sir,
The sailor lolls, with his mind at ease,
And the song and the can go quick, sir:
Laughing here,
Quaffing there,
Steadily, readily,
Cheerily, merrily,
Still from care and thinking free,
Is a sailor's life, at sea.

When the wind at night whistles o'er the deep,
And sings to the landsmen dreary,
The sailor fearless goes to sleep,
Or takes his watch most cheery:
Boozing here,
Snoozing there,
Steadily, readily,
Cheerily, merrily,
Still from care and thinking free,
Is a sailor's life, at sea.

When the sky grows black and the wind blows hard,
And the landsmen skulk below, sir,
Jack mounts up to the top-sail yard,
And turns his quid as he goes, sir:
Hawling here,
Bawling there,
Steadily, readily,
Cheerily, merrily,
Still from care and thinking free,
Is a sailor's life, at sea,

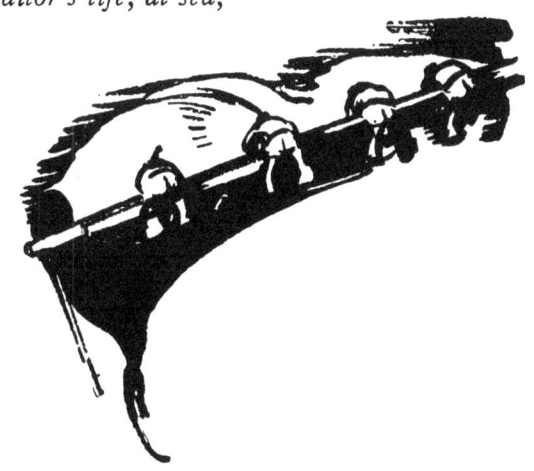

When the foaming waves run mountains high,
And the landsmen cry, "All's gone," sir,
The sailor hangs 'twixt sea and sky,
And he jokes with Davy Jones, sir!
Dashing here,
Clashing there,
Steadily, readily,
Cheerily, merrily,
Still from care and thinking free,
Is a sailor's life, at sea.

When the ship, d'ye see, becomes a wreck,
And the landsmen hoist the boat, sir,
The sailor scorns to quit the deck,
While a single plank's afloat, sir.
Swearing here,
Tearing there,
Steadily, readily,
Cheerily, merrily,
Still from care and thinking free,
Is a sailor's life, at sea.

THE DEAD HORSE

They say old man your horse will die,
And they say so, and they hope so.
Oh, poor old man your horse will die,
Oh, poor old man!

For thirty days I've ridden him,
And they say so, and they hope so.
And when he dies we'll tan his skin,
Oh, poor old horse!

And if he lives, I'll ride him again,
And they say so, and they hope so.
I'll ride him with a tighter rein,
Oh, poor old horse!

It's up aloft the horse must go,
And they say so, and they hope so.
We'll hoist him up and bury him low,
Oh, poor old horse!

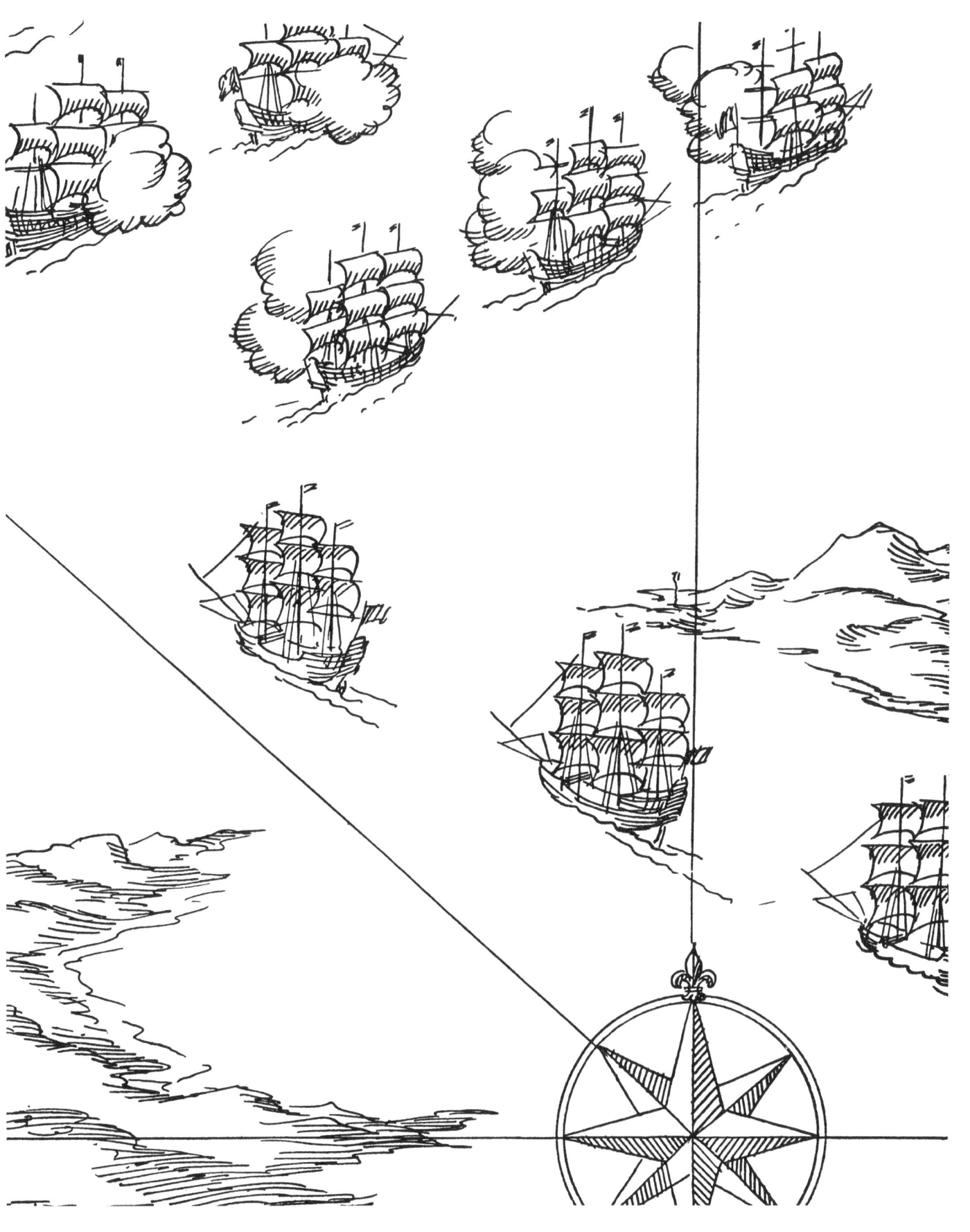

COME ROLL HIM OVER

Oho, why don't you blow?
Aha, come roll him over!
Oho, why don't you blow?
Aha, come roll him over!

One man.   To strike the bell.
Aha, come roll him over!
One man.   To strike the bell.
Aha, come roll him over!

Two men.   To take the wheel,
Aha, come roll him over!
Two men.   To take the wheel.
Aha, come roll him over!

Three men.   Top-gallant braces,
Aha, come roll him over!
Three men.   Top-gallant braces.
Aha, come roll him over!

Four men.   To man the capstan,
Aha, come roll him over!
Four men.   To man the capstan.
Aha, come roll him over!

CAPTAIN BOVER

Where have you been, my canny honey?
Where have you been, my winsome man?
I've been to the norrard,
Cruising back and forrard,
I've been to the norrard,
Cruising sore and lang.
I've been to the norrard,
Cruising back and forrard,
But I dare not come ashore,
For Bover and his gang.

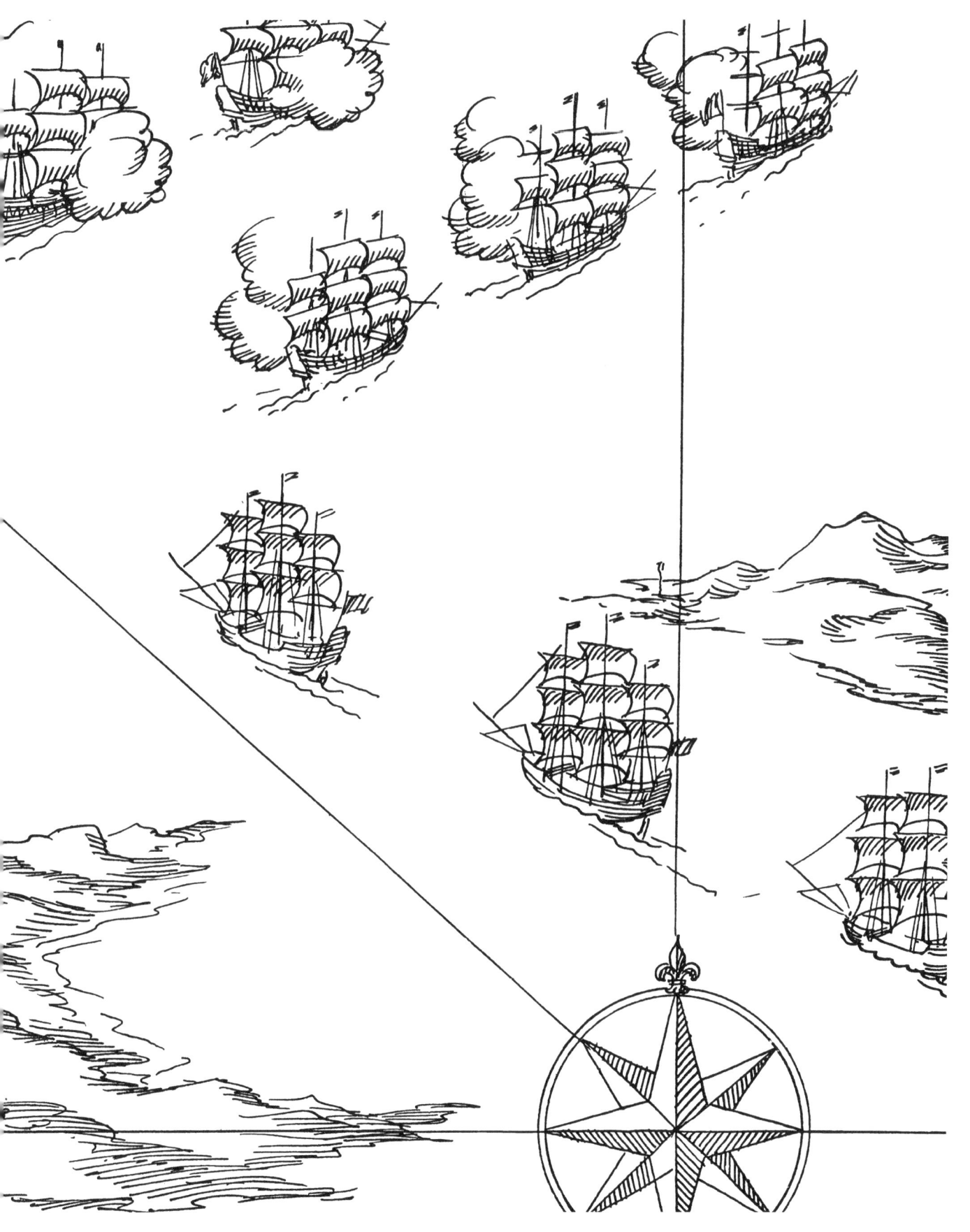

HAND OVER HAND

A handy ship, and a handy crew,
Handy, my boys, so handy;
A handy ship, and a handy crew,
Handy, my boys, away oh!

A handy skipper and second mate, too,
Handy, my boys, so handy;
A handy skipper and second mate, too,
Handy, my boys, away oh!

A handy Bose and a handy Sails,
Handy, my boys, so handy;
A handy Bose and a handy Sails,
Handy, my boys, away oh!

DOO ME AMA

As Jack was walking thro' the square,
He met a lady and a squire.
Now Jack he heard the squire say,
To-night with you I mean to stay.

Doo me ama,
Dinghy ama,
Doo me ama day.

"I will tie a string to my little finger,
And the other end hang out of the window.
Then you must come and pull the string.
I'll come down and let you in."

Doo me ama,
Dinghy ama,
Doo me ama day.

"Damn my eyes," says Jack, "if I do not venture
  To pull the string hanging out of the window."
  So Jack he went and pulled the string.
  She came down and let him in.

Doo me ama,
Dinghy ama,
Doo me ama day.

"Oh, what is this that smells so tarry?
  I've nothing in the house that's tarry;
  It's a tarry sailor down below,
  Kick him out—in the snow."

Doo me ama,
Dinghy ama,
Doo me ama day.

"Oh, what d'you want, you tarry sailor?
 You've come to rob me of my treasure."
"Oh, no," says Jack, "I pulled the string.
 You came down and let me in."

Doo me ama,
Dinghy ama,
Doo me ama day.

EARLY IN THE MORNING

Way, hay, there she rises,
Way, hay, there she rises,
Way, hay, there she rises,
Early in the morning.
What will we do with a drunken sailor?
What will we do with a drunken sailor?
What will we do with a drunken sailor?
Early in the morning.

Way, hay, there she rises,
Way, hay, there she rises,
Way, hay, there she rises,
Early in the morning.
Put him in the longboat and make him bale her,
Put him in the longboat and make him bale her,
Put him in the longboat and make him bale her,
Early in the morning.

Way, hay, there she rises,
Way, hay, there she rises,
Way, hay, there she rises,
Early in the morning.
What will we do with a drunken soldier?
What will we do with a drunken soldier?
What will we do with a drunken soldier?
Early in the morning.

Way, hay, there she rises,
Way, hay, there she rises,
Way, hay, there she rises,
Early in the morning.
Put him in the guardhouse till he gets sober,
Put him in the guardhouse till he gets sober,
Put him in the guardhouse till he gets sober,
Early in the morning.

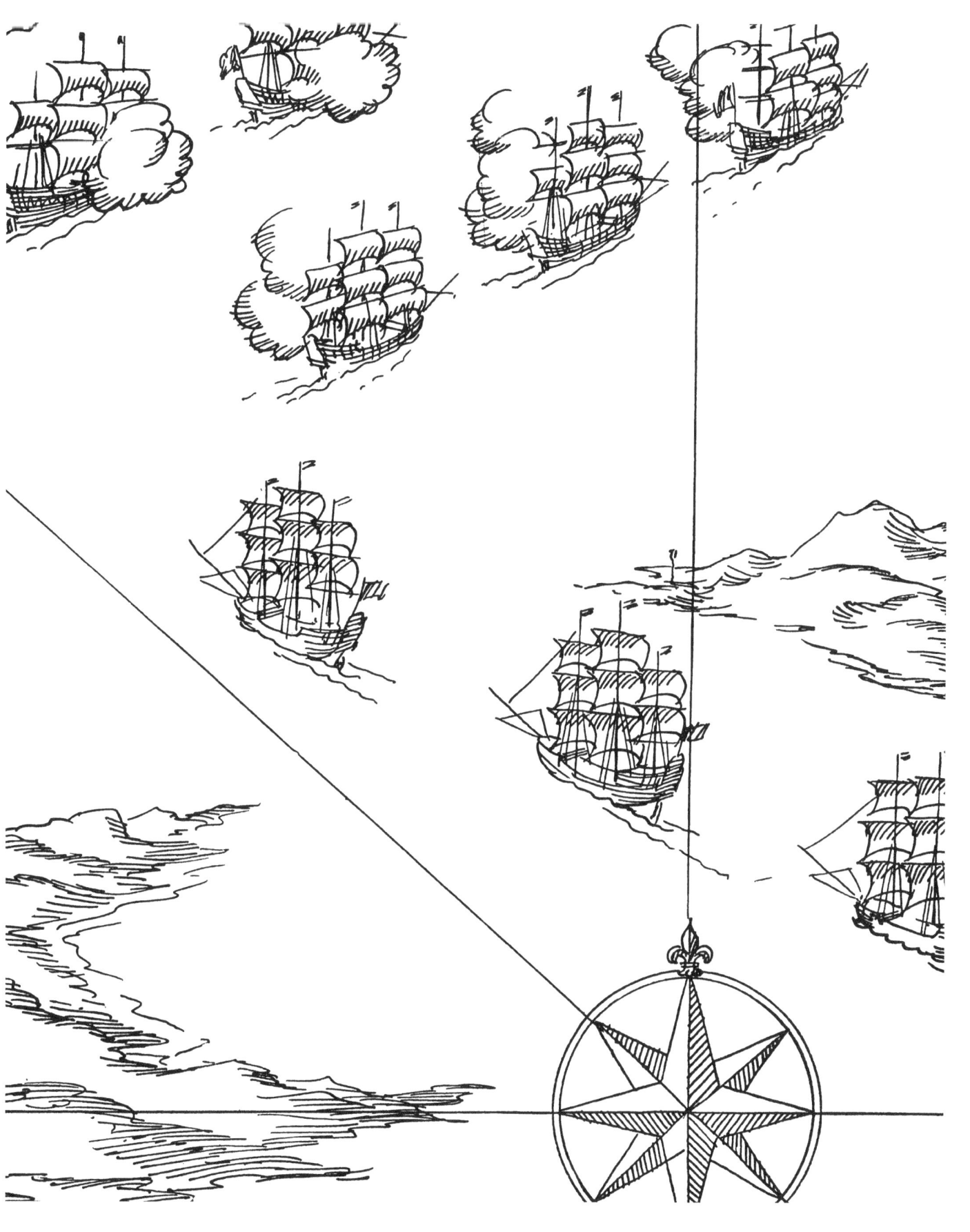

BLOW THE MAN DOWN

O blow the man down, bullies, blow the man down,
Way ay—blow the man down.
O blow the man down in Liverpool town.
Give me some time to blow the man down.

As I was walking down Paradise Street,
Way ay—blow the man down.
A brass-bound policeman I happened to meet.
Give me some time to blow the man down.

Says he, "You're a Black-Baller by the cut of your hair."
Way ay—blow the man down.
"I know you're a Black-Baller by the clothes that you wear."
Give me some time to blow the man down.

"O piliceman, O piliceman, you do me great wrong."
Way ay—blow the man down.
"I'm a *Flying Fish* sailor just home from Hong Kong."
Give me some time to blow the man down.

They gave me three months in Walton Gaol,
Way ay—blow the man down.
For booting and kicking and blowing him down.
Give me some time to blow the man down.

ACROSS THE WESTERN OCEAN

O the times are hard, and the wages low,
Amelia, whar' you bound to?
The Rocky Mountains is my home,
Across the western ocean.

That land of promise there you'll see,
Amelia, whar' you bound to?
I'm bound across that western sea,
To join the Irish army.

To Liverpool I'll take my way,
Amelia, whar' you bound to?
To Liverpool that Yankee school,
Across the western ocean.

There's Liverpool Pat with his tarpaulin hat,
Amelia, whar' you bound to?
And Yankee John the packet rat,
Across the western ocean.

Beware these packet-ships, I pray,
Amelia, whar' you bound to?
They steal your stores and clothes away,
Across the western ocean.

LOWLANDS

Lowlands, lowlands, away, my John,
Oh, my old mother she wrote to me,
My dollar and a half a day,
She wrote to me to come home from sea,
Lowlands, lowlands, away, my John.
She wrote to me to come home from sea,
My dollar and a half a day.

Lowlands, lowlands, away, my John,
A dollar a day is a Hoosier's pay,
My dollar and a half a day,
Yes, a dollar a day is a Hoosier's pay
Lowlands, lowlands, away, my John.
Yes, a dollar a day is a Hoosier's pay,
My dollar and a half a day.

Lowlands, lowlands, away, my John,
Oh, was you ever in Mobile Bay,
My dollar and a half a day,
A-screwing cotton by the day?
Lowlands, lowlands, away, my John!
A-screwing cotton by the day.
My dollar and a half a day.

THE BLACK-BALL LINE

'Twas on a Black-Baller I first served my time,
To my yeo, ho! blow the man down!
And on that Black-Baller I wasted my prime,
Oh, give me some time to blow the man down.

'Tis when a Black-Baller's preparing for sea,
To my yeo, ho!   Blow the man down!
You'd split your sides laughing at the sights you would see,
Oh, give me some time to blow the man down.

With the tinkers and tailors and soldiers and all,
To my yeo, ho!   Blow the man down!
That ship for prime seamen on aboard a Black Ball,
Oh, give me some time to blow the man down.

'Tis when a Black-Baller is clear of the land,
To my yeo, ho! Blow the man down!
Our boatswain then gives us the word of command,
Oh, give some time to blow the man down!

"Lay aft," is the cry, "to the break of the poop!"
To my yeo, ho! Blow the man down!
"Or I'll help you along with the toe of my boot."
Oh, give me some time to blow the man down!

'Tis larboard and starboard on the deck you will sprawl,
To my yeo, ho! Blow the man down.
For "Kicking Jack Williams" commands that Black Ball.
Oh, give me some time to blow the man down!

'Tis when a Black-Baller comes back to her dock,
To my yeo, ho! Blow the man down!
The lasses and lads to the pierhead do flock,
Oh, give me some time to blow the man down!

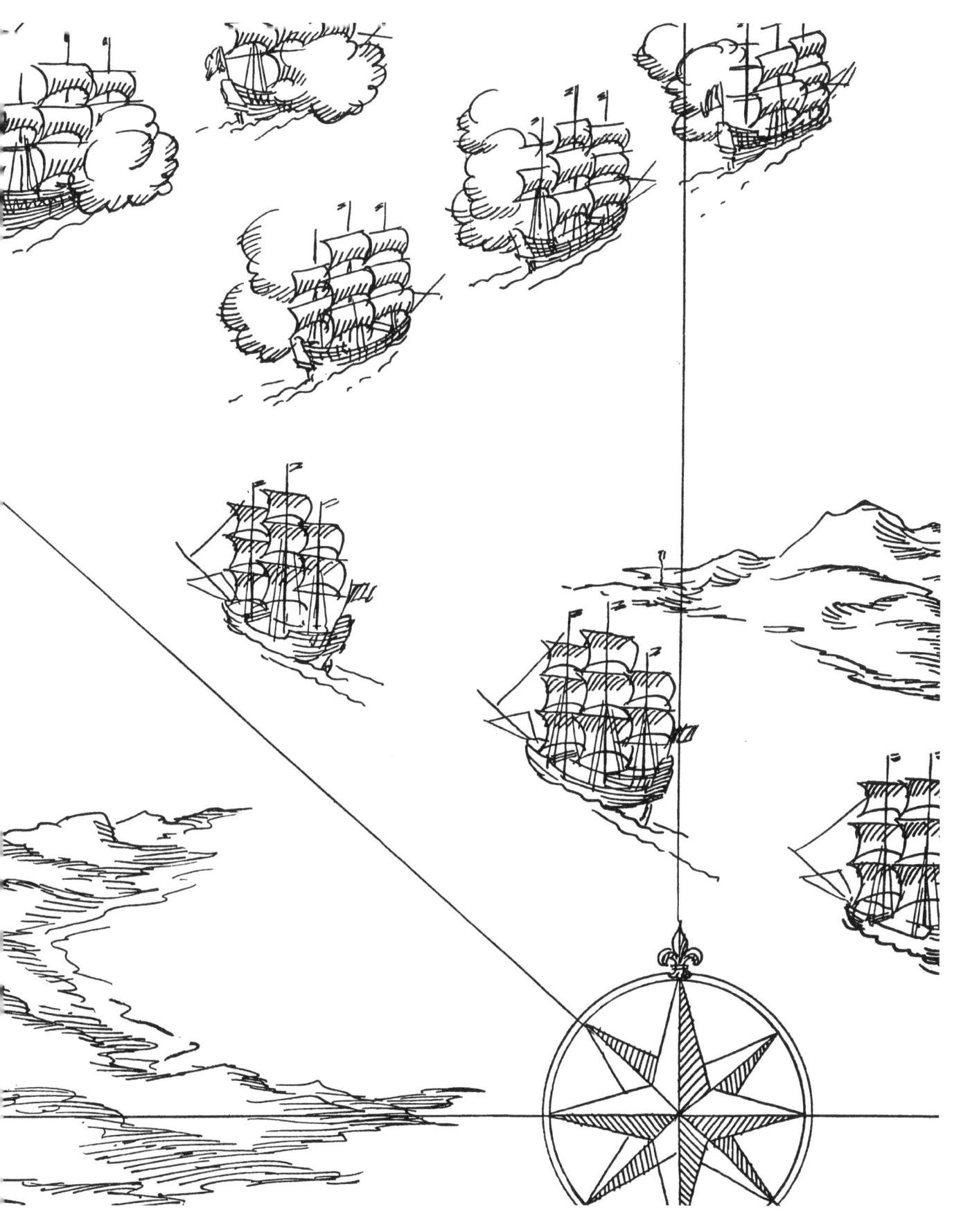

ROLL THE COTTON DOWN

Come roll that cotton, roll it down,
Oh, roll the cotton down;
Come roll that cotton, roll it down.
Oh, roll the cotton down.

I thought I heard our old man say,
Oh, roll the cotton down;
He'd sail away to Mobile Bay.
Oh, roll the cotton down.

A dollar a day is a white man's pay,
Oh, roll the cotton down;
Ten dollars a day is a black man's pay,
Oh, roll the cotton down.

Mobile Bay is no place for me,
Oh, roll the cotton down;
I'll sail away on some other sea,
Oh, roll the cotton down.

THE WIDE MISSOURI

Oh, Shenandoah, I love your daughter,
Away, my rolling river!
I'll take her 'cross yon rolling water.
Ah! ha! We're bound away
'Cross the wide Missouri.

Oh, Shenandoah, she took my fancy,
Away, my rolling river!
Oh, Shenandoah, I love your Nancy.
Ah! ha! We're bound away
'Cross the wide Missouri.

Oh, Shenandoah, I'll ne'er forget you,
Away, my rolling river!
Till the day I die, I'll love you ever.
Ah! ha! We're bound away
'Cross the wide Missouri.

THE MAID OF AMSTERDAM

In Amsterdam there dwelt a maid,
Mark well what I do say;
In Amsterdam there dwelt a maid,
And she was mistress of her trade.
I'll go no more a-roving
With you, fair maid.
A-roving, a-roving,
Since roving's been my ruin,
I'll go no more a-roving
With you, fair maid.

Her eyes were blue, her cheeks were red,
Mark well what I do say;
Her eyes were blue, her cheeks were red,
A wealth of hair was on her head.
I'll go no more a-roving
With you, fair maid.
A-roving, a-roving,
Since roving's been my ruin,
I'll go no more a-roving
With you, fair maid.

THE *GEORGE ALOE*

The *George Aloe*, and the *Sweepstake*, too,
With hey, with hoe, for and a nony no,
Oh, there were two merchantmen, a-sailing for Safee,
And alongst the coast of Barbaree.

The *George Aloe* came to anchor in the bay,
With hey, with hoe, for and a nony no,
But the jolly *Sweepstake* kept on her way,
And alongst the coast of Barbaree.

They had not sayl'd but leagues two or three,
With hey, with hoe, for and a nony no,
But they met with a French man-of-war upon the sea,
And alongst the coast of Barbaree.

"All haile, all haile, you lusty Gallants all!
  With hey, with hoe, for and a nony no,
  Of whence is your fair ship, and whither do you call?"
  And alongst the coast of Barbaree.

"We are Englishmen, and bound for Safee,"—
  With hey, with hoe, for and a nony no,
"Ay, and we are Frenchmen, and war upon the sea,"
  And alongst the coast of Barbaree.

"Amaine, Amaine, you English dogges, haile!"—
  With hey, with hoe, for and a nony no,
"Come aboard, you French swads, and strike down your sayle,"
  And alongst the coast of Barbaree.

  They laid us aboard on the starboard side,
  With hey, with hoe, for and a nony no,
  And they threw us into the sea so wide,
  And alongst the coast of Barbaree.

  When tidings to the *George Aloe* came,
  With hey, with hoe, for and a nony no,
  That the jolly *Sweepstake* by a Frenchman was ta'en,
  And alongst the coast of Barbaree.

"To top, to top, thou little Cabin-boy,
　With hey, with hoe, for and a nony no,
　And see if this French man-of-war thou canst descry,"—
And alongst the coast of Barbaree.

"A sayle, a sayle, under our lee!
　With hey, with hoe, for and a nony no,
　Yea, and another that is under her obey!"
And alongst the coast of Barbaree.

"Weigh anchor, weigh anchor, O jolly Boatswain!
　With hey, with hoe, for and a nony no,
　We will take this Frenchman, if we can,"
And alongst the coast of Barbaree.

We had not sayl'd leagues two or three,
　With hey, with hoe, for and a nony no,
　But we met the French man-of-war upon the sea,
And alongst the coast of Barbaree.

"All haile, all haile, you lusty gallants, haile!
　With hey, with hoe, for and a nony no,
　Of whence is your fair ship, and whither do you sail?"
And alongst the coast of Barbaree.

MAN OF WAR AND A CUTTER

CHINESE PIRATES

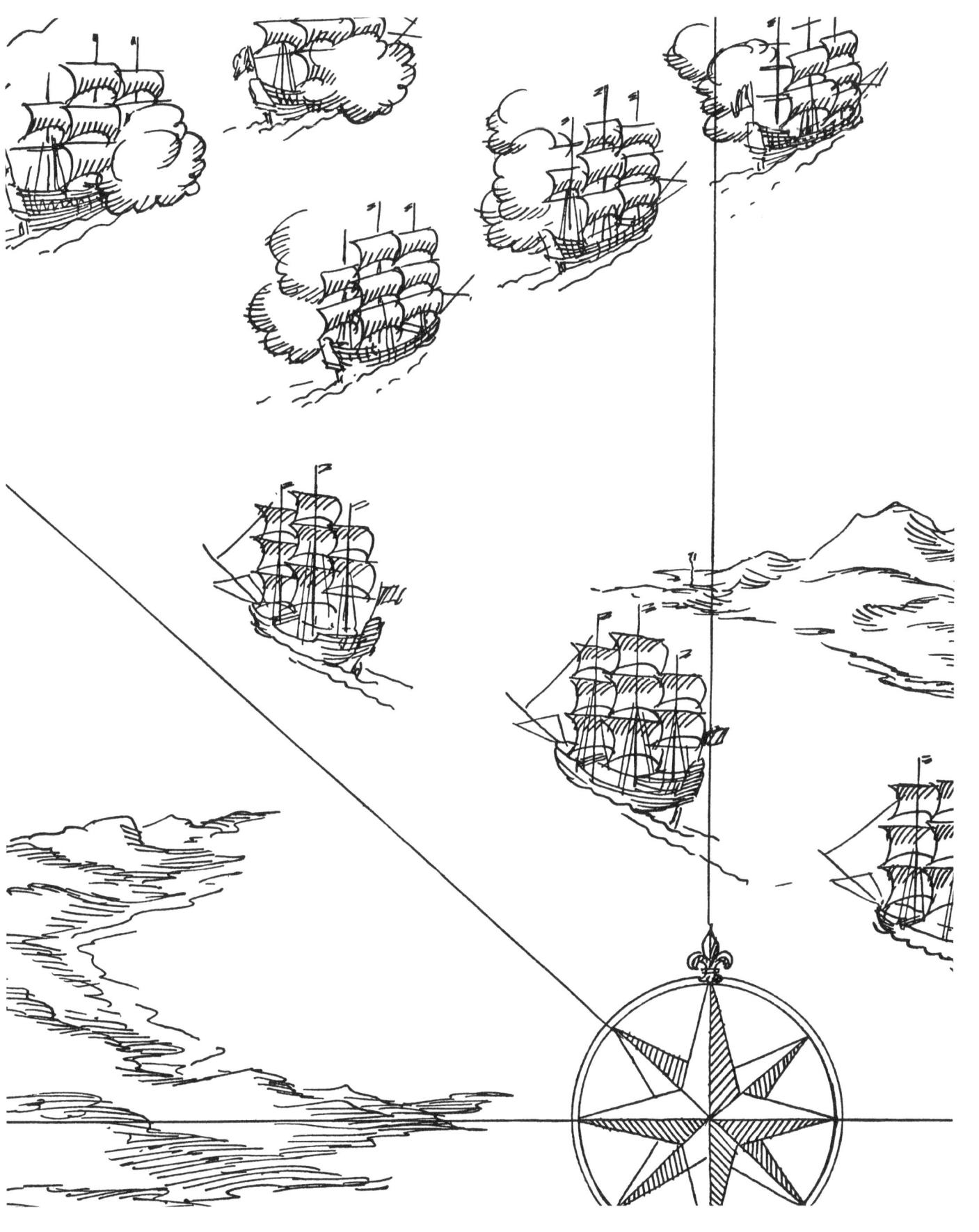

"Oh, we are merchant-men and bound for Safee,"—
With hey, with hoe, for and a nony no,
"Ay, and we are Frenchmen, and war upon the sea,"
And alongst the coast of Barbaree.

"Amaine, Amaine, you English dogges, haile!"—
With hey, with hoe, for and a nony no,
"Come aboard, you French rogues, and strike down your sayle!"
And alongst the coast of Barbaree.

The first good shot that the *George Aloe*, shot,
With hey, with hoe, for and a nony no,
He made the Frenchman's heart sore afraid,
And alongst the coast of Barbaree.

The second shot the *George Aloe* did afford,
With hey, with hoe, for and a nony no,
He struck the mainmast over the board,
And alongst the coast of Barbaree.

"Have mercy, have mercy, you brave Englishmen!"—
With hey, with hoe, for and a nony no,
"Oh, what have you done with our merry brethren?"—
As they sayl'd in Barbaree?

"We laid them aboard the starboard side,
  With hey, with hoe, for and a nony no,
  And we threw them into the sea so wide,"—
  And alongst the coast of Barbaree.

"Such mercy as you have shewed unto them,
  With hey, with hoe, for and a nony no,
  Then the like mercy shall you have again,"—
  And alongst the coast of Barbaree.

We laid them aboard the larboard side,
  With hey, with hoe, for and a nony no,
  And we threw them into the sea so wide,
  And alongst the coast of Barbaree.

Lord, how it grieved our hearts full sore,
  With hey, with hoe, for and a nony no,
  To see the drowned Frenchmen to swim along the shore!
  And alongst the coast of Barbaree.

Now gallant seamen I bid you all adieu,
  With hey, with hoe, for and a nony no,
  This is the last newes I can write to you,
  To England's coast from Barbaree.

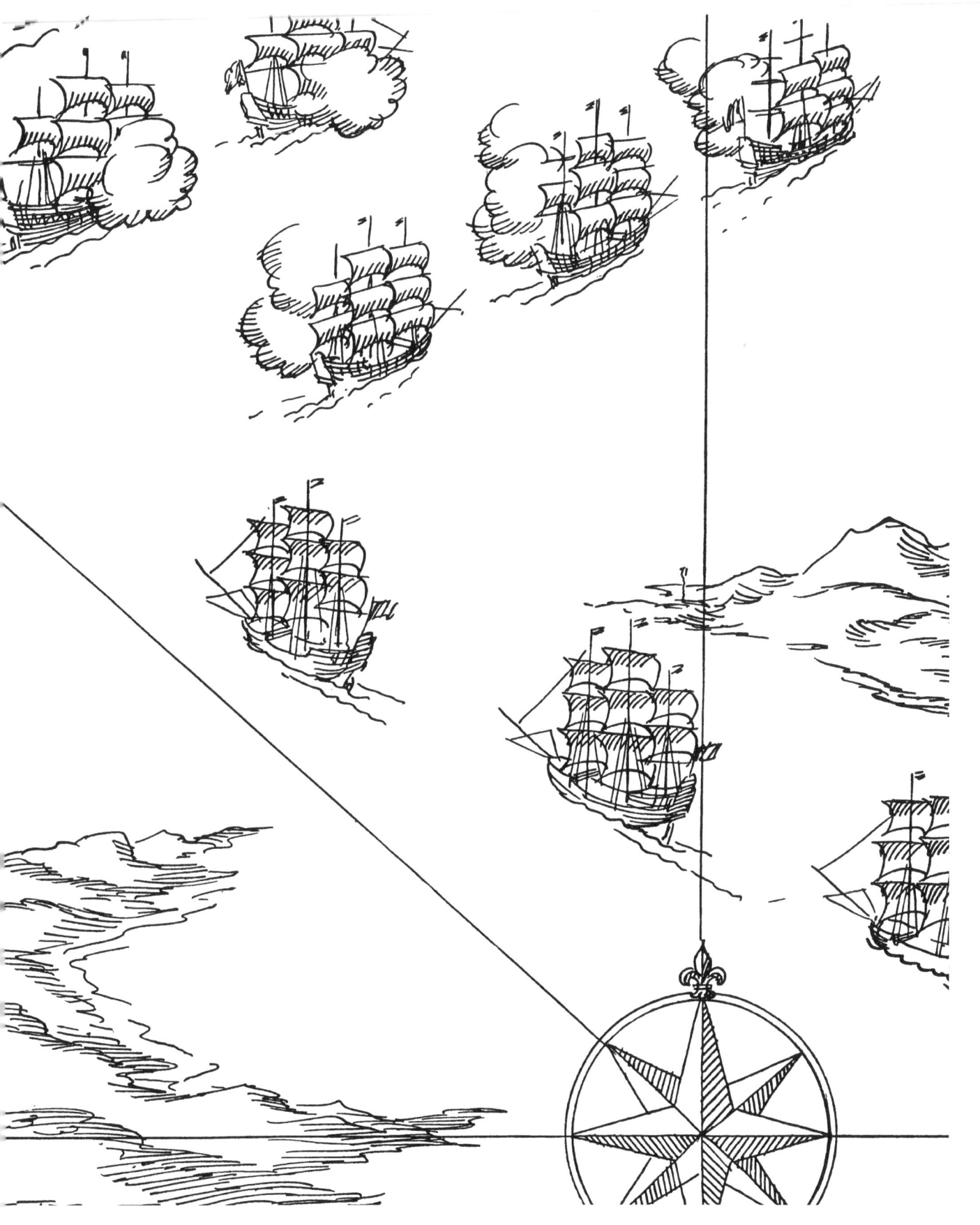

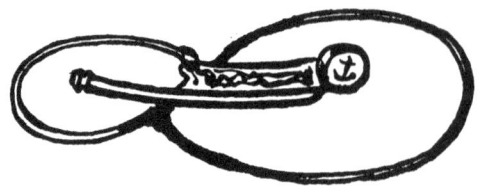

BLOW, BULLIES, BLOW

A Yankee ship comes down the river,
Blow, boys, blow!
A Yankee ship and a Yankee skipper.
Blow, my bully boys, blow!

How do you know she's a Yankee clipper?
Blow, boys, blow!
Because her mast and yards shine like silver.
Blow, my bully boys, blow!

Who do you think is captain of her?
Blow, boys, blow!
Old Holy Joe, the darky lover,
Blow, my bully boys, blow!

What do you think she's got for cargo?
Blow, boys, blow!
Why, "black sheep" that have run the embargo.
Blow, my bully boys, blow!

What do you think they have for dinner?
Blow, boys, blow!
Why monkeys' tails and bullocks' liver.
Blow, my bully boys, blow!

Oh, blow to-day and blow to-morrow,
Blow, boys, blow!
Oh, blow me down to the Congo River.
Blow, my bully boys, blow!

CAPTAIN KIDD

My name is Captain Kidd,
As I sailed, as I sailed.
My name is Captain Kidd,
As I sailed.
My name is Captain Kidd,
Many wicked things I did;
God's laws I did forbid,
As I sailed.

My topsails they did shake,
As I sailed, as I sailed.
My topsails they did shake,
As I sailed.
My topsails they did shake,
And the merchants they did quake,
For many I did take,
As I sailed.

Oh, I murdered William Moore,
As I sailed, as I sailed.
Oh, I murdered William Moore,
As I sailed.
Oh, I murdered William Moore,
And I left him in his gore,
Many, many leagues from shore,
As I sailed.

CHEER'LY, O!

Oh, haul pulley, yoe.
Cheer'ly men.
Oh, long and strong, yoe, O.
Cheer'ly men.
Oh, yoe, and with a will,
Cheer'ly men.
Cheer'ly, cheer'ly, cheer'ly, O!

A long haul for widow Skinner,
Cheer'ly men.
Kiss her well before dinner,
Cheer'ly men.
At her, boys, and win her,
Cheer'ly men.
Cheer'ly, cheer'ly, cheer'ly, O!

A strong pull for Mrs. Bell,
Cheer'ly men.
Who likes a lark right well,
Cheer'ly men.
And, what's more, will never tell,
Cheer'ly men.
Cheer'ly, cheer'ly, cheer'ly, O!

Oh, haul and split the blocks,
Cheer'ly men.
Oh, haul and stretch her luff,
Cheer'ly men.
Young Lovelies, sweat her up,
Cheer'ly men.
Cheer'ly, cheer'ly, cheer'ly, O!

SIGNALLING FOR A PILOT

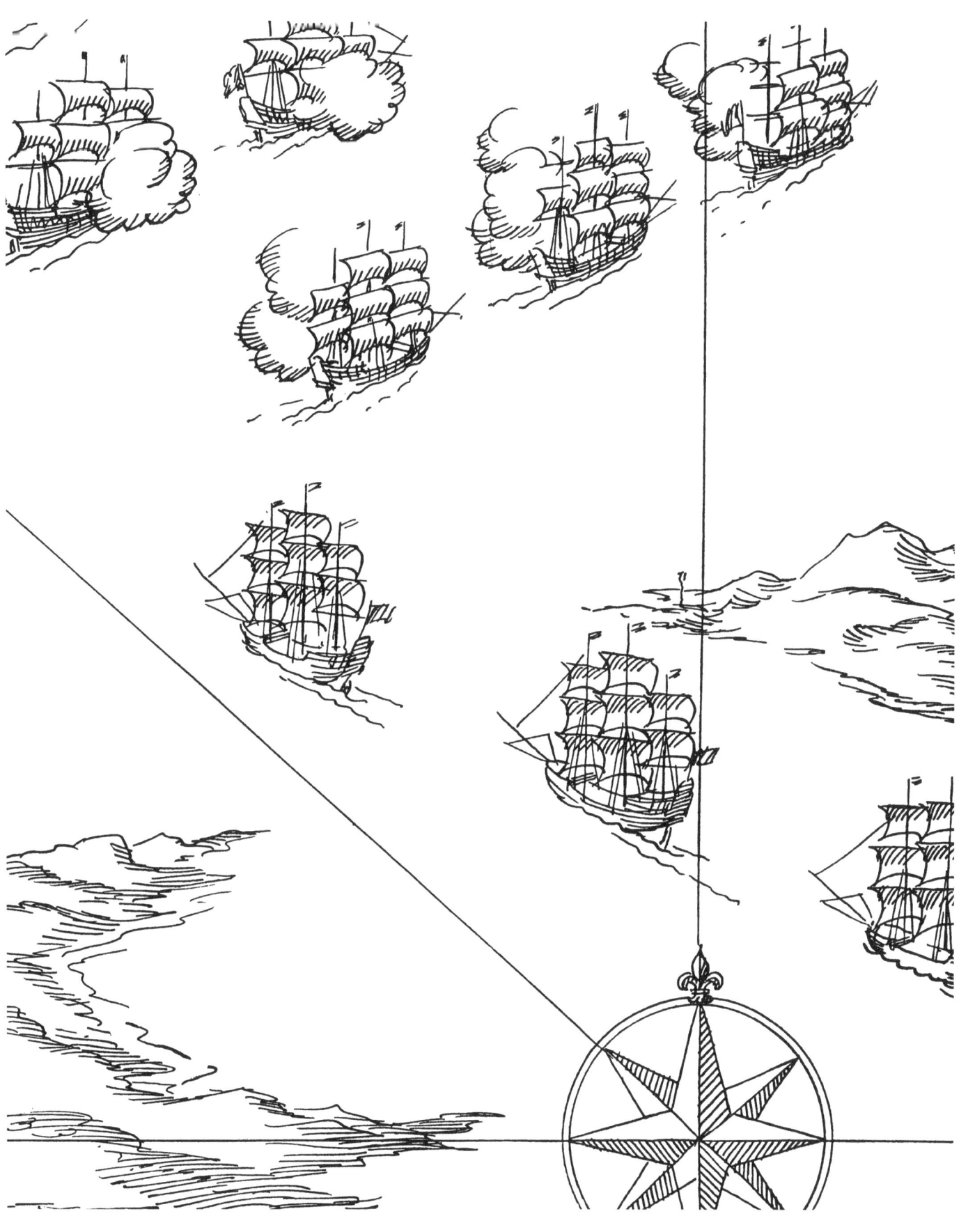

HANGING JOHNNY

They call me Hanging Johnny,
Away-i-oh;
They call me Hanging Johnny,
So hang, boys, hang!

First I hung my mother,
Away-i-oh;
Then I hung my brother,
So hang, boys, hang!

Hang and haul together,
Away-i-oh;
Hang for better weather,
So hang, boys, hang!

WHISKY FOR MY JOHNNY

Oh, whisky is the life of man,
Whisky, Johnny!
I drink whisky when I can,
Oh, whisky for my Johnny!

Whisky from an old tin can,
Whisky, Johnny!
I'll drink whisky when I can,
Oh, whisky for my Johnny!

I drink it hot, I drink it cold,
Whisky, Johnny!
I drink it new, I drink it old,
Oh, whisky for my Johnny!

Whisky makes me feel so sad,
Whisky, Johnny!
Whisky killed my poor old dad,
Oh, whisky for my Johnny!

TOMMY'S GONE TO HILO

Tommy's gone, what shall I do?
Hey-yay to Hilo!
Tom is gone, and I'll go to,
Tommy's gone to Hilo.

Oh, way round to Callao
Hey-yay to Hilo!
The Spanish gels he'll see, I know,
Tommy's gone to Hilo.

Oh, I love Tom and he loves me,
Hey-yay to Hilo!
He thinks of me, when out at sea,
Tommy's gone to Hilo.

Oh, Tommy's gone for evermore,
Hey-yay to Hilo!
I'll never see my Tom no more,
Tommy's gone to Hilo.

BONEY

Boney was a warrior,
Away-ay, ah!
A warrior, a warrior,
Jean François.

Boney beat the Prussians
Away-ay, ah!
Then he licked the Russians,
Jean François.

He went to Saint Helena,
Away-ay, ah!
There he was a prisoner,
Jean François.

SALLY BROWN

Oh Sally Brown of New York City,
Way-ay, roll and go!
Oh Sally Brown you're very pretty,
And I'll spend my money on Sally Brown.

Oh, Sally Brown's a bright mulatter,
Way-ay, roll and go!
She drinks rum and chews tobaccer,
And I'll spend my money on Sally Brown

Oh, Sally Brown's a Creole lady,
Way-ay, roll and go!
She's the mother of a yeller baby,
And I'll spend my money on Sally Brown.

Seven long years I courted Sally
Way-ay, roll and go!
Sweetest gel in all the valley,
And I'll spend my money on Sally Brown.

Seven long years and she wouldn't marry,
Way-ay, roll and go!
And I no longer cared to tarry,
And I'll spend my money on Sally Brown.

So I courted Sal, her only daughter,
Way-ay, roll and go!
For her I sail upon the water,
And I'll spend my money on Sally Brown.

Sally's teeth are white and pearly,
Way-ay, roll and go!
Her eyes are blue, her hair is curly,
And I'll spend my money on Sally Brown.

Now my troubles are all over,
Way-ay, roll and go!
Sally's married to a nigger soldier,
And I'll spend my money on Sally Brown.

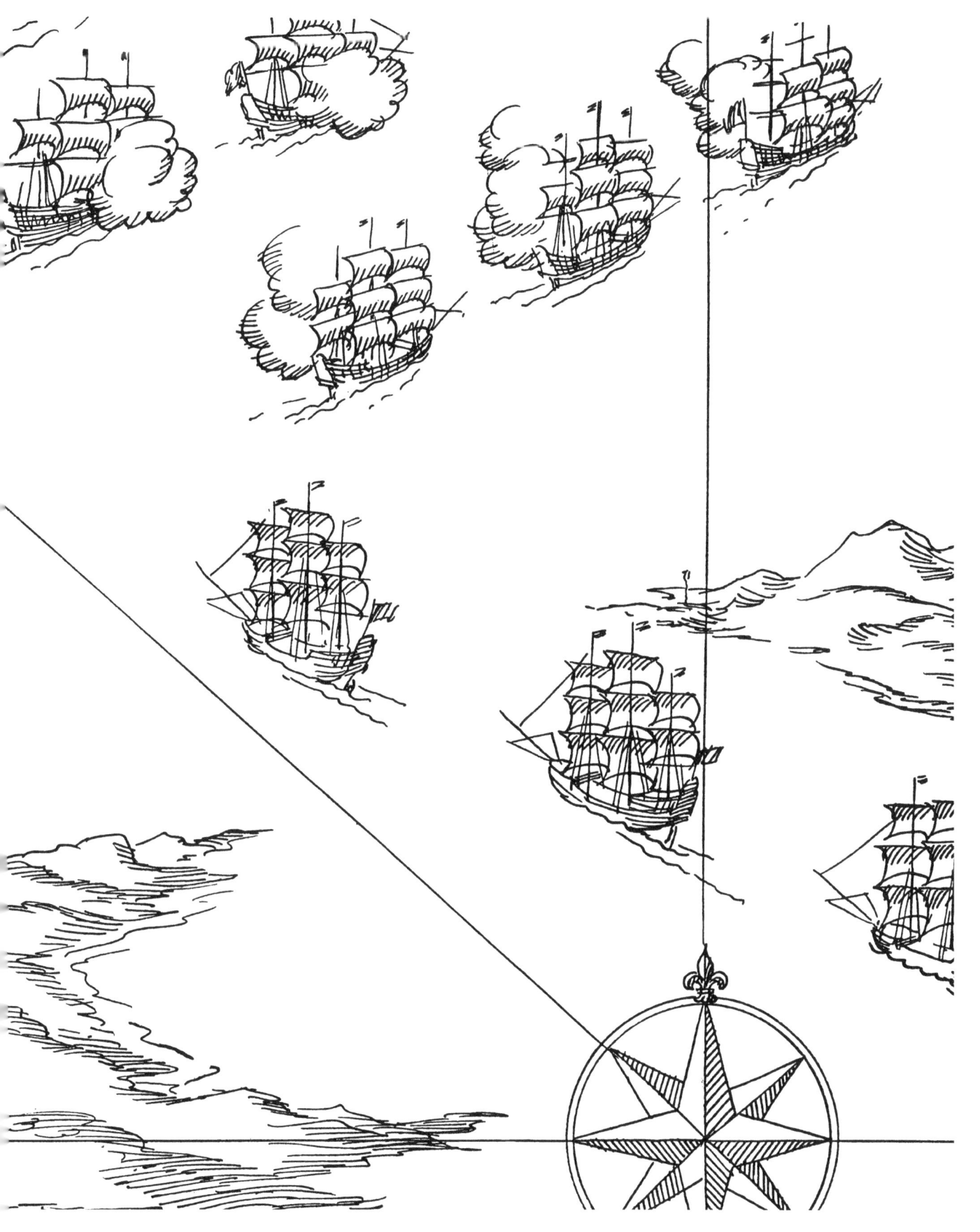

THE PLAINS OF MEXICO

Oh, Santa Anna fought for fame,

Hooray, Santa Anna!

He fought for fame and gained his name

All along the plains of Mexico.

General Taylor gained the day,

Hooray, Santa Anna!

And Santa Anna ran away

All along the plains of Mexico.

HAUL AWAY, JOE

Away, haul away, Oh, haul away together,
Away, haul away, Oh, haul away, Joe.

Once I had an Irish girl and she was fat and lazy,
Away, haul away, Oh, haul away, Joe.

But now I've got a yellow one she nearly drives me crazy,
Away, haul away, Oh, haul away, Joe.

A HEART OF OAK

THE SAILORS RETURN

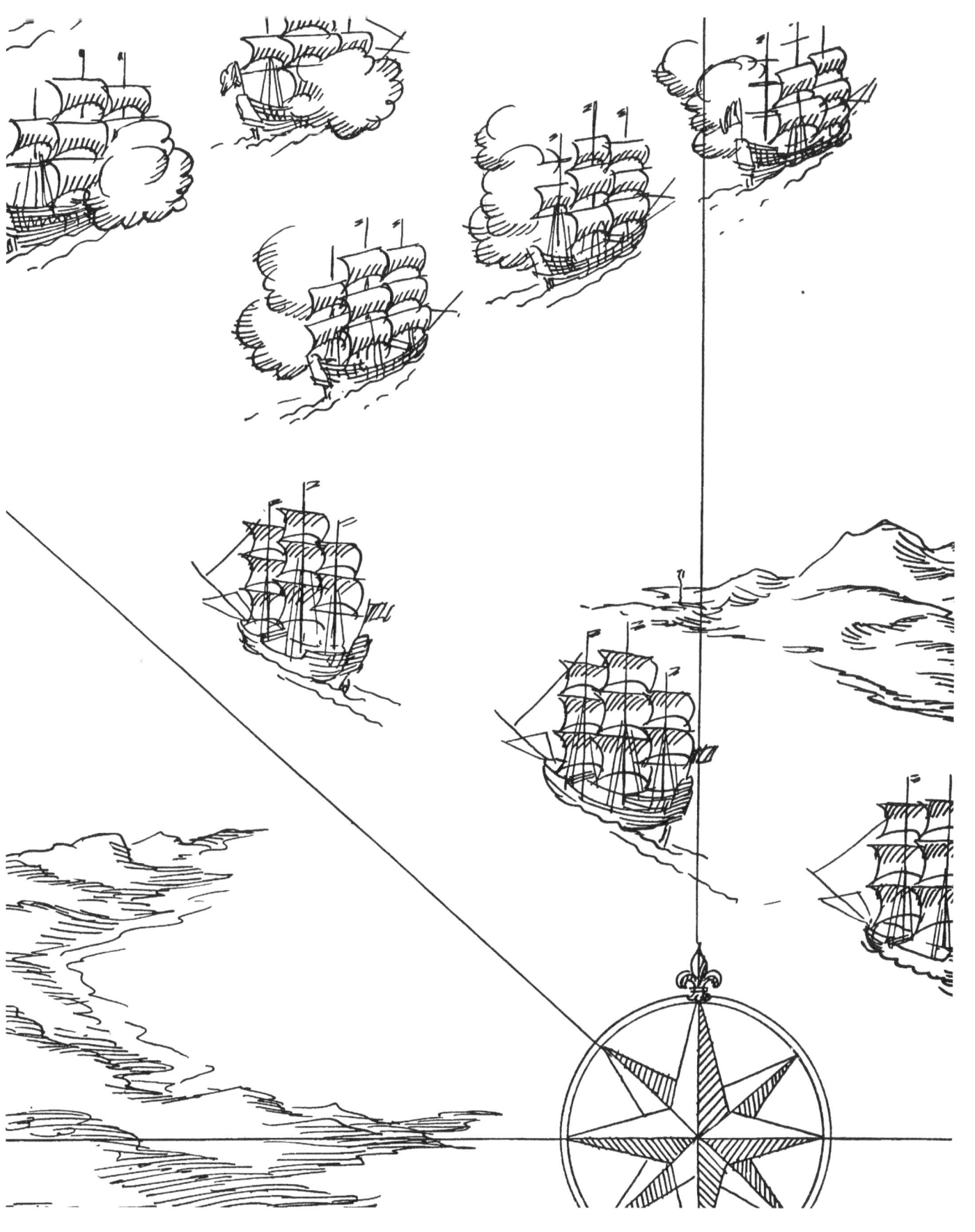

JOHNNY BOKER

Oh, do, my Johnny Boker, come roll or rock me over,
Do, my Johnny Boker, do!

Oh, do, my Johnny Boker, they say you are no rover,
Do, my Johnny Boker, do!

Oh, do, my Johnny Boker, I'm bound away to leave you,
Do, my Johnny Boker, do!

HIGH BARBAREE

There were two lofty ships from old England came,
  Blow high, blow low, and so sailed we;
One was the *Prince of Luther*, and the other *Prince of Wales*,
  Cruising down along the coast of the High Barbaree.

"Aloft there, aloft!" our jolly boatswain cries,
  Blow high, blow low, and so sailed we;
"Look ahead, look astern, look aweather and alee,
  Look along down the coast of the High Barbaree."

There's nought upon the stern, there's nought upon the lee,
  Blow high, blow low, and so sailed we;
But there's a lofty ship to windward, and she's sailing
                                                fast and free,
  Sailing down along the coast of the High Barbaree.

"Oh, hail her, Oh, hail her," our gallant captain cried,
  Blow high, blow low, and so sailed we;
"Are you a man-o'-war or a privateer," said he,
"Cruising down along the coast of the High Barbaree?"

"Oh, I am not a man-o'-war nor privateer," said he,
  Blow high, blow low, and so sailed we;
"But I'm a salt-sea pirate a-looking for my fee,
  Cruising down the coast of the High Barbaree."

  Oh, 'twas broadside to broadside a long time we lay,
  Blow high, blow low, and so sailed we;
  Until the *Prince of Luther* shot the pirate's masts away,
  Cruising down along the coast of the High Barbaree.

"Oh, quarter, Oh, quarter," those pirates then did cry,
  Blow high, blow low, and so sailed we;
  But the quarter that we gave them—we sunk them in the sea,
  Cruising down along the coast of the High Barbaree.

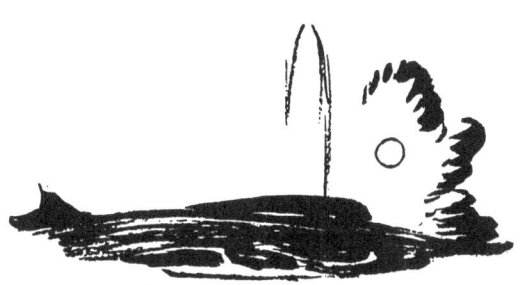

SHE BLOWS!

REUBEN RANZO

Oh, poor old Reuben Ranzo,
Ranzo, boys, Ranzo;
Oh, poor old Reuben Ranzo,
Ranzo, boys, Ranzo.

Oh, Reuben was a tailor,
Ranzo, boys, Ranzo;
He shipped on board a whaler,
Ranzo, boys, Ranzo.

But he could not do his duty,
Ranzo, boys, Ranzo,
No, he could not do his duty,
Ranzo, boys, Ranzo.

And they gave him nine and thirty,
Ranzo, boys, Ranzo,
Yes, lashes nine and thirty,
Ranzo, boys, Ranzo.

Now, the captain being a good man,
Ranzo, boys, Ranzo,
He took him in the cabin,
Ranzo, boys, Ranzo.

And he gave him wine and water,
Ranzo, boys, Ranzo,
Rube kissed the captain's daughter,
Ranzo, boys, Ranzo.

He taught him navigation,
Ranzo, boys, Ranzo,
To fit him for his station,
Ranzo, boys, Ranzo.

Now, Ranzo he's a sailor,
Ranzo, boys, Ranzo.
He's chief mate of that whaler,
Ranzo, boys, Ranzo.

He's married the captain's daughter,
Ranzo, boys, Ranzo.
And sails no more upon the water,
Ranzo, boys, Ranzo.

WE'RE ALL BOUND TO GO

Oh, as I walked down the Landing Stage
All on a summer's morn,
Heave away, my Johnnies, heave away!
It's there I spied an Irish girl
A-looking all forlorn,
And away, my Johnnie boys,
We're all bound to go!

"Oh, good morning, Mr. Tapscott,"
"Good morning, my girl," said he.
Heave away, my Johnnies, heave away!
"Have you got a packet ship
To carry me across the sea?"
And away, my Johnnie boys,
We're all bound to go!

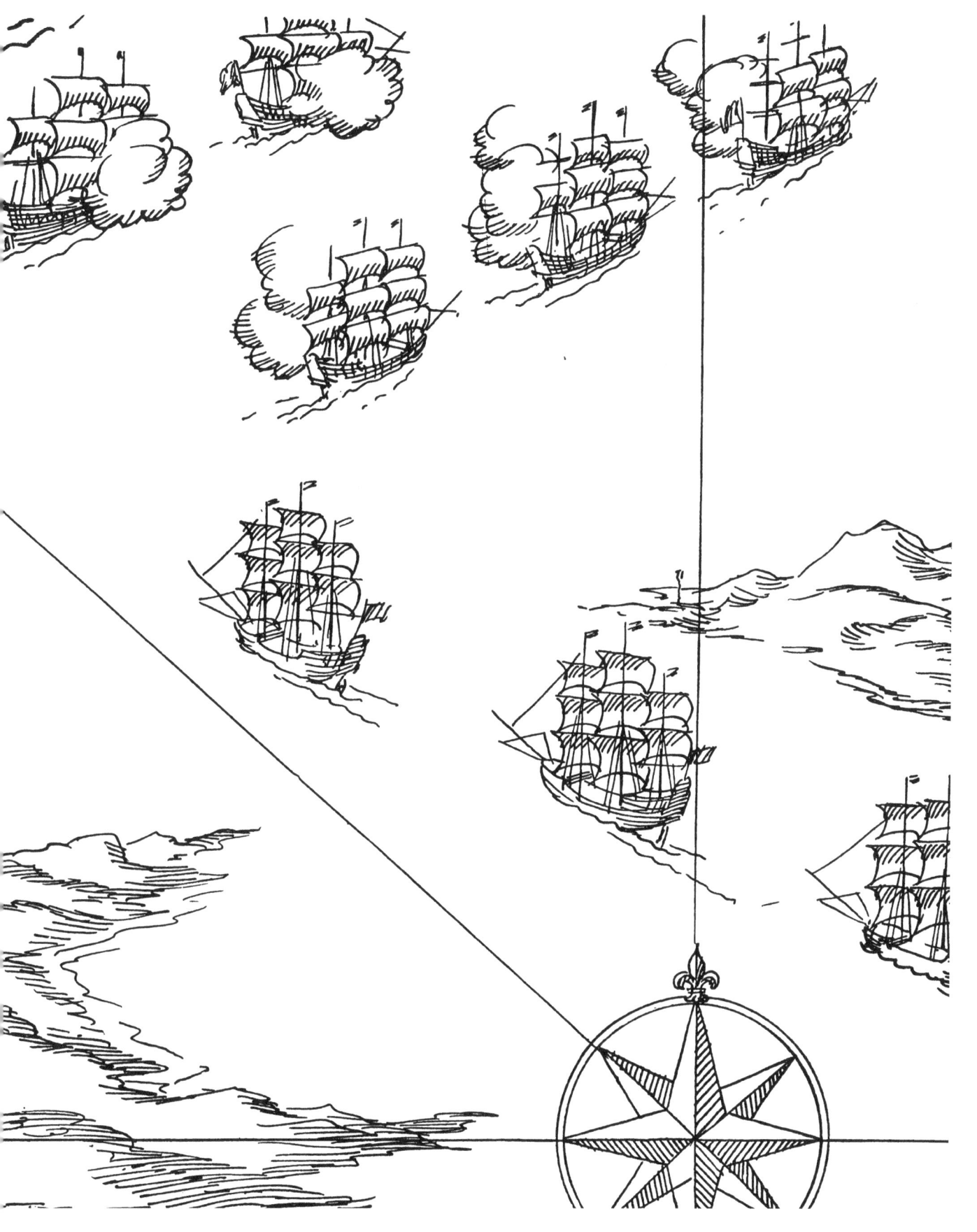

"Oh, yes I have a clipper ship,
　She's called the *Henry Clay*";
　　Heave away, my Johnnies, heave away!
"She sails away at break of day,
　She sails to-day for Boston Bay."
　　And away, my Johnnie boys,
　　We're all bound to go!

"Oh, will you take me to Boston Bay
　When she sails away at break of day?"
　　Heave away, my Johnnies, heave away!
"I want to marry a Yankee boy,
　And I'll cross the sea no more."
　　And away, my Johnnie boys,
　　We're all bound to go!

STORM-ALONG

Stormie's gone, that good old man,
To my way hay, storm along, John!
Stormie's gone, that good old man,
To my aye, aye, aye, Mister Storm-along!

They dug his grave with a silver spade,
To my way hay, storm along, John!
His shroud of finest silk was made,
To my aye, aye, aye, Mister Storm-along!

They lowered him with a silver chain,
To my way hay, storm along, John!
Their eyes all dim with more than rain,
To my aye, aye, aye, Mister Storm-along!

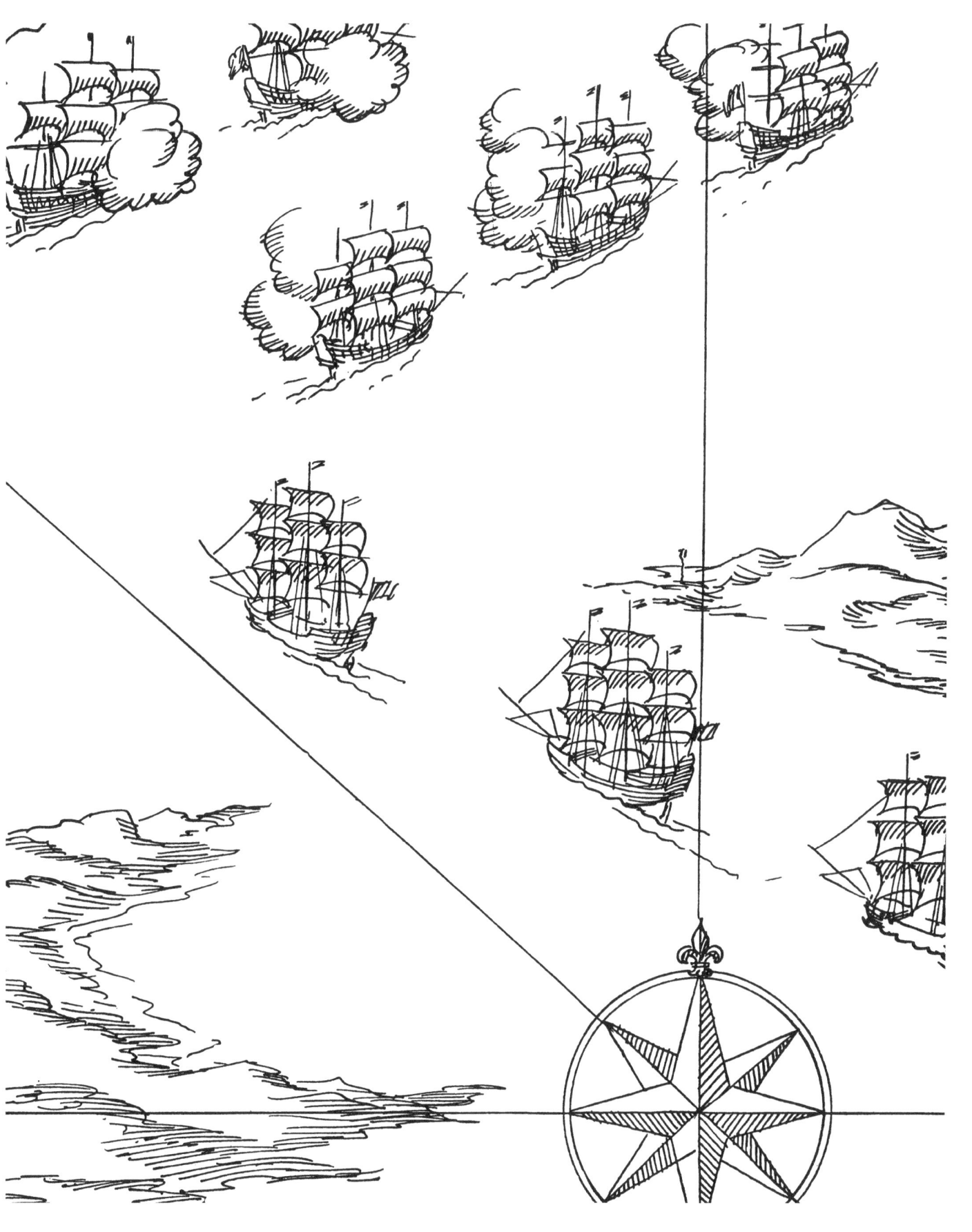

An able sailor, bold and true,
To my way hay, storm along, John!
A good old skipper to his crew,
To my aye, aye, aye, Mister Storm-along!

He's moored at last, and furled his sail,
To my way hay, storm along, John!
No danger now from wreck or gale,
To my aye, aye, aye, Mister Storm-along!

Old Stormy has heard an angel call,
To my way hay, storm along, John!
So sing his dirge now, one and all,
To my aye, aye, aye, Mister Storm-along!

PADDY DOYLE

To *my*,
Ay,
And we'll *furl*,
Ay,
And pay Paddy Doyle for his boots.

We'll *sing*,
Ay,
And we'll *heave*,
Ay,
And we'll hang Paddy Doyle for his boots.

We'll *heave*,
Ay,
With a *swing*,
Ay,
And we'll all drink brandy and gin.

A LONG TIME AGO

A long, long time, and a long time ago,
To me way hay, ohio;
A long, long time, and a long time ago,
A long time ago.

A smart Yankee packet lay out in the bay,
To me way hay, ohio;
A-waiting for a fair wind to get under way,
A long time ago.

With all her poor sailors all sick and all sore.
To me way hay, ohio;
For they'd drunk all their limejuice, and could get no more,
A long time ago.

With all her poor sailors all sick and all sad,
To me way hay, ohio;
For they'd drunk all the limejuice, and no more could be had,
A long time ago.

She was waiting for a fair wind to get under way,
To me way hay, ohio;
She was waiting for a fair wind to get under way,
A long time ago.

If she hasn't had a fair wind she's lying there still,
To me way hay, ohio;
If she hasn't had a fair wind she's lying there still,
A long time ago.

CHEER'LY MAN

Oh, Nancy Dawson, hio!
Cheer'ly man;
She's got a notion, hio,
Cheer'ly man!
For our old bosun, hio!
Cheer'ly man,
Oh! hauley, hio!
Cheer'ly man.

Oh, Betsy Baker, hio!
Cheer'ly man;
Lived in Long Acre, hio,
Cheer'ly man,
Married a Quaker, hio.
Cheer'ly man,
Oh, hauley, hio!
Cheer'ly man.

Oh, the ladies of the town, hio!
Cheer'ly man,
All soft as down, hio,
Cheer'ly man,
In their best gown, hio.
Cheer'ly man,
Oh! hauley, hio!
Cheer'ly man.

Oh, haughty cocks, hio,
Cheer'ly man,
Oh, split the blocks, hio,
Cheer'ly man,
Oh, stretch her luff, hio.
Cheer'ly man,
Oh! hauley, hio.
Cheer'ly man.

ROLL AND GO

There was a ship—she sailed to Spain,
Oh, roll and go!
There was a ship came home again,
Oh, Tommy's on the topsail yard!

What d'ye think was in her hold?
Oh, roll and go!
There was diamonds, there was gold.
Oh, Tommy's on the topsail yard!

And what was in her lazareet?
Oh, roll and go!
Good split peas and bad bull meat.
Oh, Tommy's on the topsail yard!

Many a sailorman gets drowned,
Oh, roll and go!
Many a sailorman gets drowned.
Oh, Tommy's on the topsail yard!

POOR OLD JOE

Old Joe is dead and gone to hell,
Oh, we say so, and we hope so;
Old Joe is dead and gone to hell.
Oh, poor old Joe!

He's as dead as a nail in the lamp-room door,
Oh, we say so, and we hope so;
He's as dead as a nail in the lamp-room door.
Oh, poor old Joe!

He won't come hazing us no more,
Oh, we say so, and we hope so;
He won't come hazing us no more,
Oh, poor old Joe!

"I AM A BRISK AND SPRIGHTLY LAD"

I am a brisk and sprightly lad,
But just come home from sea, sir.
Of all the lives I ever led,
A sailor's life for me, sir.

Yeo, yeo, yeo,
Whilst the boatswain pipes all hands,
With a yeo, yeo, yeo!

What girl but loves the merry tar,
We o'er the ocean roam, sir,
In every clime we find a port,
In every port a home, sir.

Yeo, yeo, yeo,
Whilst the boatswain pipes all hands,
With a yeo, yeo, yeo!

But when your country's foes are nigh,
Each hastens to his guns, sir.
We make the boasting Frenchmen fly,
And bang the haughty Dons, sir.

Yeo, yeo, yeo,
Whilst the boatswain pipes all hands,
With a yeo, yeo, yeo!

Our foes reduc'd, once more on shore,
We spend our cash with glee, sir.
And when all's gone we drown our care,
And out again to sea, sir.

Yeo, yeo, yeo,
Whilst the boatswain pipes all hands,
With a yeo, yeo, yeo!

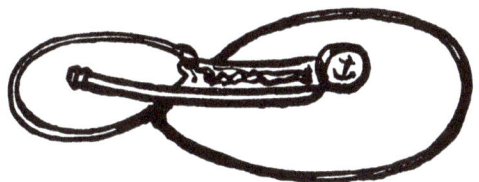

BEN BACKSTAY

Ben Backstay was a boatswain,
A very jolly boy,
No lad than he more merrily
Could pipe all hands ahoy.
And when unto his summons
We did not well attend,
No lad than he more merrily
Could handle a rope's end.

Singing chip cho, cherry cho,
Fol de riddle ido,
Singing chip cho, cherry cho,
Fol de riddle ido.

It chanced one day our captain,
A very jolly dog,
Served out to all the company
A double share of grog.
Ben Backstay he got tipsy,
Unto his heart's content,
And being half-seas over,
Why overboard he went.

Singing chip cho, cherry cho,
Fol de riddle ido.
Singing chip cho, cherry cho,
Fol de riddle ido.

A shark was on the larboard bow:
Sharks don't on manners stand,
But grapple all they come near,
Just like your sharks on land.
We heaved Ben out some tackling,
Of saving him in hopes;
But the shark he bit his head off,
So he couldn't see the ropes.

Singing chip cho, cherry cho,
Fol de riddle ido.
Singing chip cho, cherry cho,
Fol de riddle ido.

Without his head his ghost appeared
All on the briny lake:
He piped all hands aloft, and said;
"Lads, by me warning take:
By drinking grog I lost my life,
So, lest my fate you meet,
Why, never mix your liquors, lads,
But always drink them neat."

THE BANKS OF THE SACRAMENTO

Sing and heave, and heave and sing,
To me hoodah! To my hoodah!
Heave and make the handspikes spring.
To me hoodah! To me hoodah!
And it's blow, boys, blow,
For Californi—o.
For there's plenty of gold,
So I've been told,
On the banks of the Sacramento.

From Limehouse Docks to Sydney Heads,
To me hoodah! To my hoodah!
Was never more than seventy days.
To me hoodah! To me hoodah!
And it's blow, boys, blow,
For Californi—o.
For there's plenty of gold,
So I've been told,
On the banks of the Sacramento.

ON LEAVE

We cracked it on, on a big skiute,
To me hoodah! To my hoodah!
And the old man felt like a swell galoot.
To me hoodah! To me hoodah!
And it's blow, boys, blow,
For Californi—o.
For there's plenty of gold,
So I've been told,
On the banks of the Sacramento.

HAUL THE BOWLINE

Haul on the bowlin', the fore and maintop bowlin',

Haul on the bowlin', the bowlin' haul!

Haul on the bowlin', the packet is a-rollin',

Haul on the bowlin', the bowlin' haul!

Haul on the bowlin', the skipper he's a-growlin',

Haul on the bowlin', the bowlin' haul!

Haul on the bowlin', to London we are goin',

Haul on the bowlin', the bowlin' haul!

Haul on the bowlin', the good ship is a-bowlin',

Haul on the bowlin', the bowlin' haul!

Haul on the bowlin', the main-topgallant bowlin',

Haul on the bowlin', the bowlin' haul!

GOOD-BYE, FARE YOU WELL

Oh, fare you well, I wish you well!
Good-bye, fare you well; good-bye, fare you well!
Oh, fare you well, my bonny young lassies,
Hurrah, my boys, we're homeward bound!

Oh, don't you hear our old man say
Good-bye, fare you well; good-bye, fare you well!
We're homeward bound this very day?
Hurrah, my boys, we're homeward bound!

We're homeward bound, and I hear the sound,
Good-bye, fare you well; good-bye, fare you well!
So heave the capstan and make it spin round.
Hurrah, my boys, we're homeward bound!

Our anchor's aweigh and our sails they are set,
Good-bye, fare you well; good-bye, fare you well!
And the gels we are leaving we leave with regret.
Hurrah, my boys, we're homeward bound!

She's a flash clipper packet and bound for to go;
Good-bye, fare you well; good-bye, fare you well!
With the gels on her tow-rope she cannot say no.
Hurrah, my boys, we're homeward bound!

HOMEWARD BOUND

Now to Blackwall Docks we bid adieu,
To Suke, and Sal, and Kitty, too,
Our anchor's weighed, our sails unfurled,
We are bound to plough the watery world.
Huzza, we're homeward bound!

Now the wind blows hard from the east-nor'-east,
Our ship she sails ten knots at least,
The purser will our wants supply,
And while we've grog we will ne'er say die.
Huzza, we're homeward bound!

And should we touch at Malabar,
Or any other port as far,
Our purser he will tip the chink,
And just like fishes we will drink.
Huzza, we're homeward bound!

And now our three years it is out,
It's very near time we back'd about,
And when we're home, and do get free,
Oh! won't we have a jolly spree.
Huzza, we're homeward bound!

And now we haul into the docks,
Where all those pretty gels come in flocks,
And one to the other they will say,
"Oh! here comes Jock with his three years' pay!"
Huzza, we're homeward bound!

And now we haul to the Dog and Bell,
Where there's good liquor for to sell,
In comes old Archer with a smile,
Saying, "Drink, my lads, it's worth your while,
For I see you are homeward bound."

But when our money's all gone and spent,
And none to be borrowed nor none to be lent,
In comes old Archer with a frown,
Saying, "Get up, Jock, let John sit down,
For I see you are homeward bound."

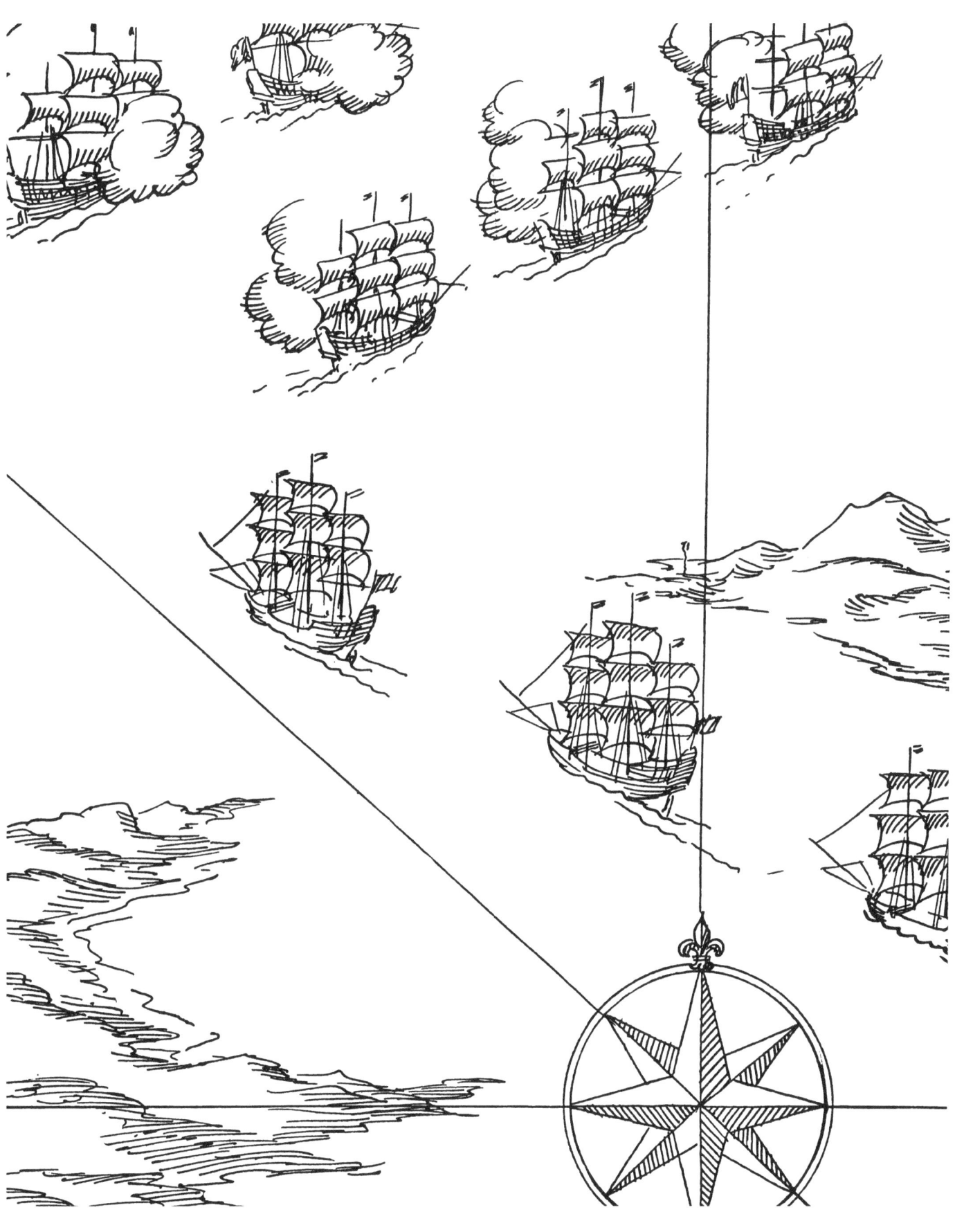

ONE DAY MORE

Only one day more, my Johnny,
One more day?
Oh, rock and roll me over,
Only one more day!

Oh, don't you hear the old man roaring?
One more day?
Oh, don't you hear that pilot bawling?
Only one more day!

Can't you hear those gels a-calling?
One more day?
Oh, can't you hear that capstan pawling?
Only one more day!

Then put on your long-tailed blue, my Johnny,

One more day?

For your pay is nearly due, Johnny.

Only one more day!

Only one day more, my Johnny,

One more day?

Oh, rock and roll me over.

Only one more day!

ROLLING HOME TO MERRIE ENGLAND

Call all hands to man the capstan,
See the cable run down clear,
Heave away, and with a will, boys,
For old England we will steer;
And we'll sing a cheerful chorus
In the watches of the night,
And we'll sight the shores of England
When the gray dawn brings the light.

Rolling home, rolling home,
Rolling home across the sea;
Rolling home to dear old England,
Rolling home, dear land, to thee.

Up aloft amid the rigging,
Blows the loud exulting gale,
Like a bird's wide outstretched pinions
Spreads on high each swelling sail;
And the wild waves cleft behind us,
Seem to murmur as they flow,
There are loving hearts that wait you
In the land to which you go.

Rolling home, rolling home,
Rolling home across the sea;
Rolling home to dear old England,
Rolling home, dear land, to thee.

Many thousand miles behind us,
Many thousand miles before,
Ancient ocean heaves to waft us
To the well-remembered shore.
Cheer up, Jack, bright smiles await you
From the fairest of the fair,
And her loving eyes will greet you
With kind welcomes everywhere.

Rolling home, rolling home,
Rolling home across the sea;
Rolling home to dear old England,
Rolling home, dear land, to thee.

IT'S TIME FOR US TO LEAVE HER, JOHNNY

I thought I heard the skipper say,
Leave her, Johnny, leave her!
To-morrow you will get your pay,
It's time for us to leave her.

The work was hard, the voyage was long,
Leave her, Johnny, leave her!
The seas were high, the gales were strong,
It's time for us to leave her.

The food was bad, the wages low,
Leave her, Johnny, leave her!
But now ashore again we'll go,
It's time for us to leave her.

The sails are furled, our work is done,
Leave her, Johnny, leave her!
And now on shore we'll have our fun,
It's time for us to leave her.

NOTES

Away Rio! Capstan chanty.

A-cruising We Will Go. From Douce's "Collection of English Songs in Bodleian," Vol. I.

Spanish Ladies. From Dixon's "Ancient Poems, Ballads and Songs." This song, with variations, found great favour with the men on the clipper ships.

Jack the Guinea Pig. From Douce's "Collection," Vol. V.

The Dead Horse. A long drag or halyard chanty. When the sailor signs on he is given a month's pay in advance which is spent before the ship sails. "The Dead Horse" is the thirty days he must work before he begins to draw pay.

Come Roll Him Over. A long-drag chanty.

Captain Bover. Captain Bover was head of a notorious press gang.

Hand Over Hand. Hand over hand used in bringing hawse lines, etc., on board.

Doo Me Ama. A great favourite with clipper ship crews. The sailor is always in his own eyes a great lover.

Early in the Morning. A runaway chorus.

Blow the Man Down. A long-drag chanty. The equivalent of the word "blow" is knock. A variation of the theme may be found in "The Black-Ball Line."

Across the Western Ocean. A hauling chanty. Whall dates this 1850. It was current during the great Irish invasion. The name Amelia is probably a contraction of O'Melia, or O'Malley.

Lowlands. A capstan chanty. This version is an example of the type wherein the chanty is begun with the chorus. It is of American origin.

The Black-Ball Line. A long-drag chanty. The Black-Ball Line was a famous English packet fleet notorious for its brutal officers.

Roll the Cotton Down. A long-drag chanty of Southern American origin. There was great complaint among the seamen because 'longshoremen, whom they considered inferiors, were paid higher wages.

The Wide Missouri. A capstan chanty. Sometimes called *Shenandoah.* Variations: Mizzourah; Shanandore.

The Maid of Amsterdam. An old favourite that has found a resting place in many home song books. Sometimes called "*A-roving.*"

The "George Aloe." A song of the fight between the *George Aloe* and *Sweepstake* and certain French men-o'-war. *Amaine, Amaine*—strike your colours. *Swads* = swabs; sea menials.

Blow, Bullies, Blow. A long-drag chanty.

Captain Kidd. These are the regulation verses of an old sea song. The verses are interminable and the result of the sailors' improvisation.

Cheer'ly O! A long-drag chanty.

Hanging Johnny. A long-drag chanty.

Whisky for My Johnny. A long-drag chanty.

Tommy's Gone to Hilo. A hauling chanty. Some versions have it Ilo. This seems to mean little more than a signal. In the subsequent verses the ports were changed to fit in with the ship's schedule: a good chanty-man could take his crew around the world.

Boney. A long-drag chanty. *Boney* was Napoleon Bonaparte. *Jean François:* John Franswar.

Sally Brown. A capstan chanty. One of the most popular and still sung on deep-water ships.

The Plains of Mexico. A capstan chanty. This chanty commemorates the battle between the American forces under General Taylor and the Mexicans under Santa Anna. The latter were defeated, but partisanship permitted changing the words to—

And Gin'ral Taylor run away,
He ran away at Monterey.

Haul Away, Joe. A short-drag chanty.

Johnny Boker. A short-drag chanty.

High Barbaree. An old sea ballad that survives in the home song books.

Reuben Ranzo. A long-drag chanty.

We're All Bound to Go. A short-drag chanty.

Storm-Along. A pumping chanty.

Paddy Doyle. Used aloft in smothering sail and furling the bunt on the yard.
Variations:
> *We'll all drink brandy and gin*
> *We'll hang Paddy Doyle for his boots*

A Long Time Ago. A long-drag chanty.

Cheer'ly Man. A walkaway chanty.

Roll and Go. A long-drag chanty.

Poor Old Joe. A long-drag chanty. Another version of "The Dead Horse."

"I Am a Brisk and Sprightly Lad." From Douce's "Collection," Vol. II.

Ben Backstay. A ballad still sung by old sailors.

The Banks of the Sacramento. An example of the sailor's use of a minstrel ballad. The original was "The Camptown Races," an early Christy Minstrel song.

Haul the Bowline. A short-drag chanty.

Good-bye, Fare You Well. A capstan chanty.

Homeward Bound. An English version of an old ballad. Still heard on British ships.

One Day More. A pumping chanty.

Rolling Home to Merrie England. The favourite version of a modern song.

It's Time for Us to Leave Her, Johnny. A long-drag chanty.

PRINTED IN THE UNITED STATES OF AMERICA

www.ingramcontent.com/pod-product-compliance
Lightning Source LLC
Chambersburg PA
CBHW081506040426
42446CB00017B/3414